5 Minutes

VRINDA SINGH

BlueRose Publishers

First Published in December 2019

ISBN: 978-93-89763-38-6

Price: INR 199/-

BLUEROSE PUBLISHERS
www.bluerosepublishers.com
info@bluerosepublishers.com
+91 8882 898 898

Cover Design:
Vandana Kanyal

Typographic Design:
Sonia Suyal

Editor:
Ojasvee Garg

Distributed by: BlueRose, Amazon, Flipkart, Shopclues

Dedication:

For my mother, who taught me to fly,
For my brother, who weeps with me when I cry,
For friends, who are the stars of my sky,
For women, who are determined to try.

FOREWORD

Touching lives, expanding the horizons of our concern, being authentic, and always ready to share. That is not just a regular love story, it is a vivid description of some of the the most sensitive and amazing people I have encountered.

While they, perhaps live and work in different countries and different fields, share the philosophy of emotions. This book captures that philosophy and shows that it is not just a fable or a pipe dream. It is real, a situation that most of the women face in their daily lives. The book is dedicated to all the women who face difficulty in living freely because of the social norms.

Things I like about this book:

1. Fresh story: While reading I couldn't predict what is going to happen next. Twists and turns keep the reader hooked.

2. Good pace: Flow of the story is good. Facts are revealed at the appropriate intervals.

3. Romance and Mystery : Romantic thriller will keep the readers adhere to the book until end and keep giving them goosebumps.

'5 Minutes' is a must-read book, and Vrinda is committed to make it a worthy read for all the readers across the globe.

— **Ojasvee Garg** (BlueRose Editor)

Always Inspired by

—**"Ruskin Bond"**

PREFACE

Before, you begin reading this book, I would like to acknowledge that several episodes of the book are based on true incidents. All the characters in this story are fictitious. Any resemblance to any character dead or alive is completely unintentional and regretted. I don't tend to hurt the sentiments of any sect or religion or community or group. In my travels across India, I am often in search of vignettes of women, which appears to be breathing on its own. William Shakespeare had always been my greatest ideal, and I am so moved by his authored play, "Julius Ceaser", that I have added an excerpt of one of its famous, Antony's speech, in the beginning chapter.

The corporate industry background set up in the story, is most prevalent in India, still in 21st century, where most of the working women claim to be independent.

Although, my book is intended purely for entertainment of young ladies and gentleman, I hope it will not be shunned by working professionals on that account, for part of my plan was to pleasantly remind the working women about their respectful rights and also for the teenagers to understand the practicality of love, rather than getting carried away into it.

Nothing on this earth is stronger than a woman, we are just a realization behind. Writing the truth is hard, but understanding it, is very easy.

ACKNOWLEDGEMENT

This book has been extensively supported by my corporate teacher and friend Mr. Vicky Baliyan. Without his support, researching through a corporate woman's life, was almost impossible.

I thank my mother, Geeta Singh, for her patient support and my younger brother, Anshuman Singh, for being my potion, throughout the writing journey. My grandparents, Mr. Dhan Pal Singh Chauhan and Mrs. Soorajkali Chauhan, were huge source of inspiration while capturing the real episodes of the book.

My heartfelt thanks to my teacher, Mr. S. K. Agrawal for blessing me to fight all the odds. This work was ostensibly supported by my friends, whom I thank for their useful suggestions.

AUTHOR BIO

Vrinda, the author of the prime selling book "Murky Girl" boomerangs to captivate us with her new romantic thriller "5 minutes".

The founder of the country's biggest writing platform "Paperwiff", a technocrat at a reputed MNC, an entrepreneur, a speaker and a vehement blogger, Vrinda has revolutionised the country's literary status quo by reaching the mass youth and cracked wide open their writing skills, providing them with a perfect platform to effectuate their literature dreams.

What makes her idiosyncratic from the writers of her age group is her finesse of writing in vicissitude has emerged as not just perspicacious but also is an elucidation to the present-day injustice, prejudices and miseries which is the desperate need of the society.

Such is the pleasure of reading her is that the writer does it all like it is a beautiful sonnet with an inkling of Shakespeare.

Vrinda, through her world-wide followed blog "In the heat of the moment", is on a venture to capture the obscured unheard voices and liberalise them to the biggest possible audience. The Gold medalist in VLSI, Vrinda tries to actualise the same by juxtaposing modern literature and technology. In conjunction with her multifarious savvy, the young Post-graduate Vrinda is also a member of the advisory board of a reputed Govt. University and has a research paper attributed to her name.

: @authorvrinda

: @authorvrinda1

: www.intheheatofthemoment.net

: www.authorvrinda.com

CONTENTS

CHAPTER-1
REVENGEFUL ANGER

I killed the person I was in love with three years back. My dilated pupils and breathlessness is proof of my fear. Not the fear of going behind the bar but the fear of losing my beloved forever in the wake of a commitment that I could never make. The promise of holding his hands forever and never leaving his side is parked somewhere in stark loneliness. The air of betrayal, today, is wild enough to destroy the happy home which we made three years ago in the heart of the country, Delhi. Today is 15th August

2019, the Independence day of India. While every citizen is celebrating India's liberation, I am observing unwanted freedom. The words of love are resonating through my ears, cluttering all that I am trying to hear.

Yes, I am happy that I don't have to suffocate my aspirations anymore. Yes, I am free today to live my life on my own terms and conditions. I feel liberated. But, yes, I am in sheer pain of losing him. There is something about him which is compelling me to bring him back. His touch reverberates through my skin, impacting every single cell of my body. His pretty and small eyes, even when closed, could see me at my best. I still feel as if he is watching me and smiling because of those eternal five minutes; I am spending with him. All that started in five minutes, ended in five minutes.

I am sitting down on the floor of his old house, trembling underneath hatred and ignorance. And, he is lying next to me— motionless, ready to question my absence from his death. I still can't believe that I have killed him, the person whom I love. My heart plunges in abject misery today, bleeding in the sorrow of murdering the one who was the best in his humour. Antony in Julius Caeser rightly said, "The evil that men do lives after them; the good is oft interred with their bones." I am here to sing in his praise after suffering at the hands of a possessive mind. Perplexed in satirical love, I can't detach my soul from his. He was a kind soul but a lousy lover. The room is small and is suffocating as the doors and windows of the room are tightly closed. I am struggling for breath. I need water to wet my dry lips which are murmuring in the hope of hearing from him. I still can't reckon that I have turned into a murderer.

Everything seems alive— the furniture, the curtains, the fridge and the walls, but he is dead.

His lively pictures on the wall seem to be talking to me, questioning me, "Why aren't you with me, Pooja? Why did you leave me, Pooja?"

His perfume is still lingering in my senses. He would pour bottles on himself to make sure that his body odour stays covered. He loved me a lot, yet I butchered my love. I want to pee, but I can't leave him alone here. He would get angry. I wish I could wake him up and ask him to accompany me to the washroom. The insoluble dilemma of loneliness didn't spare me any time to let me rush to the nearest pothole. I have finally peed in my pants. I am just staring at him, lying by his side, holding his hand in this sordid condition. I am slowly falling in the deep slumber of the golden old days that I had spent with him, murmuring Jeeva! Jeeva! Jeeva!

The day of Janmashtmi, a festival in India, where the entire country prepares to celebrate the birthday of Lord Krishna, the God with an enormous number of personalities. I woke up early morning in the holiest city of the country, Varanasi. School days are over now, and I am an IIT and MBBS aspirant. Nothing fancy like movies. I don't wake up every day facing river Ganges. My life was as average as a girl next door. I lived in the narrow city lanes with a beautiful mother and an uncaring father. I didn't have siblings with whom I could share my joys and sorrows. My mother has always been my ideal, inspiring me to fight all the odds without making any noise. My father was the one who neglected me the most, from childhood obstinacy to adulthood advice. I was a little different when it came to achieving things. Not really a bookworm by nature, I had this uncanny habit of relishing what I read, which made me stand out. Mother, being a teacher by profession, and father, being a businessman, couldn't spend quality time with me. I was a loner with creative ideas.

In the blink of an eye, I had lost half of my preparation time in my tortoise approach of cracking either JEE or MBBS. My father left no stone unturned to get me married and get rid of me completely, but my mother is heaven-sent. She saved me from all the social perils. Today is Janmashtmi; I am excited to celebrate Lord Krishna's birthday. I always wondered if true love like that of Lord Krishna and Radha's exists. Not in my case, at least. I never felt the love till date. So, the doctrine of love was merely an imaginative entity for me. Assisting my mother with the daily chores and rifling through the storeroom to get the best dresses for Lord Krishna. The city is chanting the divine songs. All I am seeking is a stable career in either of the two streams.

Medical, Ummm, doesn't really suit me. I am meant for the corporate world. Pondering the exciting new career ahead, I dreamt with my eyes wide open. High heels, short skirts and a fancy handbag, what else could a small-town girl wish for? Glasshouse with stylish windows and designer curtains, and suddenly my angry mother knocks my head, "Always daydreaming! Could you please, get back to work and help me with the preparation of sweets. Today's kids, I swear, listen to no one. We were such obedient kids in our time." The rant wouldn't stop till I gathered the utilities for Lord Krishna while assisting her in preparing sweets. The long day is over and I am damn hungry. It's still 8

PM. Four long hours to go for Lord Krishna to unveil his cute little naughty face. With a tired look, I peep out of my window to see little kids playing in the streets.

Childhood is a thing to adore, we don't realise it until we grow up to hold the mountains of responsibilities. I was so carefree in those kitty days. Yet another call from my mother, "Pooja, you better start decorating the worship place in the house. It's already nine." I coldly replied with drooping shoulders and a big sigh, "Yes, mom. Coming." The live telecast of Krishna Janmashmti is the news of the day. From televisions to radio stations, people are talking about Lord Krishna. The clock struck 12, and we all sang, "Radhey Radhey, Hail Lord Krishna". Mother lit a candle in front of baby Lord Krishna to welcome him on earth and prayed him to steal all our pains. We all joined hands and bowed down in respect and happiness of having him amongst us. Variety of sweets and food were served around the little God in the joy of his arrival. I obediently picked all of the vessels of savoury to the dining table. We finished by 1:00 AM, and I laid deep in my bed.

CHAPTER 2
A NEW WORLD

The next morning was four months later, which started with exam anxiety and ended with a sigh of relief as the exams met their destination. I share every experience with my mother. She is my best friend since childhood. With limited friends, as I mentioned that I am an introvert, I always wondered how interesting it would be to have a conversation with a boy. But, the boys around still sucked or you can say I never mustered the courage to let anyone approach me. My father had never been a man I could look up to. Unlike every other girl, my father was never my superhero. Every time I buzzed him, he would shoo me off bluntly.

I stopped minding him when I was four, and he never minded me at all. It's January 2014, and I am all set to apply for colleges. As I anticipated, I was going to be a corporate girl because of engineering. Breaking the barriers, a small-town girl was entering a superfast dream city. My happiness knew no bounds when I was awarded a scholarship for scoring the highest in the entrance exam. Instructions from the college were quite hard for me, but the exhilaration of joining a college and living independently had lit hopes of achieving what I always wanted to. I packed my entire luggage and stuffed my bags with the miscellaneous I tried to carry. Starting a new journey was daunting, and I was all geared up to become an ardent traveler. The astoundingly huge campus with jaw-dropping ambience had already convinced me that I was at the right place. I was a meritorious student since school, so the fear of spending 4 long years here wasn't bothering me at all. While the other kids were making merry with new introductions, I was busy skimming and scanning the library. Never ever had I seen such a vast library. It made my heart gasp. "This is my new home", I said appreciating myself for getting enrolled in one of the Delhi's best colleges. After all, I deserved self-praise for I have managed to start my career on a good note. Hostels were neat and tidy, and I was content with the no room-sharing arrangements made by the administration. 'Fabulous, it's just me and my books. I live my way, I stay my way. I like it. Good job, Pooja.' The first day of the college was a calling challenge. Girls of my section locked me up in the washroom while I had a new shower experience. "Knock, Knock! Who locked me?

Take me out, please? I will miss my class. It's my first day",
I shouted with a frown.

Alas! My screeches didn't work, and I sat drumming
the door. asking for help when suddenly, the receptionist
came to my rescue. She unlocked the door and asked for
my health. To which I cried, "First, find out who locked
me. I have missed my first class." I rushed to the room of
my dreams, gathering my belongings. Fortunately, I was on
time for the second period but all the girls from my class
started laughing the moment I entered the classroom. I was
shrewd enough to understand that this act of felony must be
the wicked plot of one of them who was giggling. "Never
mind, Pooja! Every dog has its day", I murmured to myself
again.

Every other day, something weird would happen to me.
Sometimes, imprisoned in the washroom and sometimes,
robbed of my notebooks, the level of frustration was soaring
high like Delhi's temperature in June. No matter what I tried
the girls of my class didn't gel well with me. It was a matter
of grave concern for me. I didn't know what I have done
wrong to the 28 girls in my course to make them not like
me. Well, I wasn't as ugly as you are imagining right now.
I had no sense of doing makeup but, at least, I had a better
understanding of carrying myself. The college's beautiful
and serene campus gave me all the time and opportunities
to explore and make the best of my imagination. Lush green
trees, an artificial lake, a gigantic library; life had never
bestowed anything better than this before.

It's been more than one year in college now. I have
established myself as a meritorious student, caged in her

room all day, sometimes writing, sometimes studying and sometimes indulging in creative activities. Life was on a smooth roll, except friends. Like every other regular guy or girl, I had no friends. Had this situation been evitable, I could have plucked the stars for it. I used to call my mother thrice a week and update her about the latest happenings. She would always advise me to try to bridge the gap between the other girls and me. But all my efforts were futile. It's rightly said in India, "There can be delays at God's place but not darkness."At the culmination of every semester, girls from my branch and also from different departments would queue up in my room to seek suggestions on the question paper patterns. The overweening ego of the girls would go down the slop at the end of every semester. I anticipated the comradeship of girls, every time I helped them with their assignments and exams doubts. But poor me! As far as the boys are concerned, I found nobody worthy of me. Going by the facts, I knew my engagements and commitments to my work wouldn't let me spend time with my loved ones, albeit even 5 minutes are sufficient in a relationship. Isn't it? I spoke to myself again.

So, one not-so-long-year at college has already passed in discomfort. I have slowly deciphered the reason behind the backbiting. One day, I was surprised when I was interrupted by Jai, the first-ever guy of the class who politely said, "Excuse Me" after a year. To which I, too, broke my silence and whispered shyly, "Hey Jai! How are you doing?" Jai smiled and offered me a walk to my hostel. Well, I couldn't deny him that, and we started strolling in small steps. "You are such a meritorious student, why don't you talk in class?"

I was saddled by his presence as it has never happened in my life that I would to a guy without pretext. "Ummm... I just don't feel comfortable with guys around, and my efforts of making a treaty with the girls are all wasted." "Why do they hate me so much?", I frowned. Jai took a pause and answered, "It is because you keep yourself reserved and the guys of the class like you a lot. But, since you are a tough nut, nobody dares to talk to you." A spring smile appeared on my face, and I didn't utter a word. We reached the destination, and he said goodbye to me.

I am delighted today. This not-so-shoddy feeling about Jai was persistent for days now. The good thing is that we are making news with his friends in the class. I see a drastic change in the girls' behaviour too. They have started talking to me. "I didn't know, a five minutes conversation with you will change my life entirely", I told Jai on the coffee table in the cafeteria. Jai giggled and robbed my hairband, trying to catch hold of some fun. Ad interim, a girl, named Sakshi has been stealing my personal space since Jai started talking to me. Sakshi is my classmate and has been showing a great interest in being my friend. Those five minutes were magical enough to enchant the people around me.

People have finally started liking me. Sakshi, Jai and I were making a perfect tripartite. From group studies to evening snacks, we were glued to each other. The college life looked precisely like a filmy college life, after a year. But, not all fingers are the same and the day arrived when Jai called me out for dinner. I asked Jai on call, "So, where are we three hunting this Saturday night?". He whispered, "It's just you and me".

I chided, "What?????"He exclaimed, "Ah, come on. She is visiting her parents this Saturday".

"Alright. Let's go then," I replied. This is a long weekend. Sakshi and majorly all the hostel residents were travelling back to their home. I was an abandoned kid, so family visits for me were prohibited. Since I was studying on scholarships, paying for my tuition fee wasn't much of a concern for my parents. However, mom would send some Rs. 500/- for my monthly expenses. The day arrived. Dressed up in casual jeans and a T-shirt, Jai and I hired an auto around 8 PM and reached an Indian restaurant not very far from our residential area. It was a small round table, topped with a neat table cloth, accessorised with a candle and a rose flower. We were facing each other on our comfortable chairs, and Jai was looking at me awestruck. "Is there something you want to point out? Do I look weird? This lost look on your face is irritating me Jai," I jittered. Jai nodded his head left and right possessively and answered, "Are you a fool? Don't you understand why we are here on a candlelight dinner? Pooja, please don't act smart. It's been a month since we have been dating now and I am getting this cold response from you. At least try to be a little romantic." I didn't know what to say. I picked up my bag and called an auto to go back to the hostel. Jai followed me, screaming, "Pooja, Pooja, Poo.... "

My intense sobbing sounds were echoing around the corner of the hostel, but there was no one to hear me out or console me. Jai has dropped some 100 unanswered calls on my phone since the moment I left him at the restaurant. I locked myself up and switched off my phone for the entire Sunday, trying to figure out yesterday's episode. 'Jai is in love with me. No, this can't happen. He is my best friend but hell no; he can't fall in love with me'. Upset with everything around, on Monday morning, I knocked on Sakshi's door with a freckled face. Sakshi unlatched the door asking, "What's wrong, Pooja, you look scared?" I replied, "Jai is in love with me". Sakshi angrily replied, "Are you crazy? Jai belongs to me. I am in love with him since the first year. Just get out of my room. I knew you were intelligent in studies, but since when you have started using your intellect in stealing boyfriends. Get out right now and don't dare talk to me or cross my way ever." Sakshi pushed me out of the room and thrashed the door.

CHAPTER-3
LUST IN DISGUISE

I with a lost look, unable to decipher what was going on around me, sat outside Sakshi's room for an hour, pondering the way out of this situation. Time has again turned the table. I have lost my best friend in the wake of love. The love that I never felt. I had no idea that the passion that started with a five-minute conversation would end up like this. I left Sakshi's room and went for a solitary walk in the campus, missing all my classes, weeping, sobbing and questioning life for this surprise pain. After spending almost the entire day outside, I returned back to my hostel. At the hostel, life was normal, girls were giggling, watching TV, teasing each other, and I was quiet inside, upset and lost in the pace of relationships. I was unlocking my room when I heard something from behind. "Pooja, Jai wishes to talk to you. He is on call," Sakshi uttered, handing over the phone to me. I stammered and said, "Hello, Jai. I......" And, Jai interrupted me and said, "Pooja, you will regret not valuing my love. Life is a bitch, and your karma will come back to you. I am glad that at least Sakshi loves me and she expressed her possessiveness for me. I curse you for not finding love ever. I don't wish to speak to you or see you ever."

"Jai...Jai...but........" I expressed in between the disconnected call tone.

"It's all over Pooja. You have lost us forever. I will make sure that no girl in my gang talks to you ever," shouted Sakshi.

My long face with tears rolling down entered the room. leaving behind a deafening bang of the door. I am all alone again. But what did I do wrong? I was questioning myself again and again. I wept the entire night, thinking about what life has in store for me. I wanted to cry out loud and seek out a friend. This was the loneliest moment of my life ever. I shunned myself from everything. I knew books were the only friends I could make merry with. Every day, I would just walk out of the hostel to the class and back to the hostel again. Sakshi boycotted me in the girls' hostel, and Jai wouldn't even look at me in the class. It is so reckless to be deprived of love and care. Weekends used to be super lonely, patrons visit their juveniles, and I used to stare at those long crowded corridors, waiting for somebody I know. Mom used to be super busy picking up fights with my dad and earning for my pocket money.

I could focus well on my studies because I couldn't let my empty brain clatter. Securing the first position in my class was the only option I was left with. My love for literature started growing. If not with a person, then, with Julius Ceaser, the hero of all times. If I had a chance to bring one person back to life, it would be Julius Ceaser. The classic, Julius Ceaser, became the essence of my life. I was playing the role of Brutus, who couldn't be friends either with Julius or Casca, trying to follow the truth, yet ended up messing up things. I was participating in everything I never wanted to do. From sports to marathon, from exhibitions to acts and plays, I was just trying to escape reality. Medals and trophies are replacing the void of my life, albeit meaningless to me. I had established a name for myself but was yearning for someone I could count on. Fall exams are approaching, I am all geared up to chase a good score with my intense preparations. It was the lab verification exam on the first day. The lab assistant was distributing question papers to the class. Suddenly, I seemed to forget the concepts I had memorised. Jai and Sakshi spread the rumour that most of the questions are out of syllabus. I took a deep breath of satisfaction for I was not the only one who was facing the dolour in answering the questions. Harpreet, the naughtiest of the class, managed to open up the book and spread the circulars of a few correct answers across the level.

I was panicking; my legs were shaking with anxiety. I cursed myself for not mugging up the entire book by heart. One hour had already passed, and the students in the lab were moving around those small answer chits to get the passing marks. I was waiting if anyone would share the chit with me, though I was against cheating, the adrenaline was pulsating. I was eagerly waiting for someone to hand over the small paper to me. Ten more minutes have already gone, but none came to my rescue. Students of my class have finally started retreating from the examination lab. I was sitting, shaking up my legs vigorously in sheer anxiety. Last five minutes were left before the examiner would snatch away the sheets when I got the small answer chit in my hand. The teardrop was a 'thank you' to that hand which passed it over to me. I raised my head above and saw that it was the lab examiner. I dropped the paper shivering in extreme fear.

"I am so sorry, sir. I didn't mean to copy any answer. Excuse me!" I murmured in fear. Ravinder, the lab assistant, giggled and said, "I am offering these answers to you, and I have written the answers of all the questions. I won't tell anybody, and I assure you *'Excellent'* Grade in this exam." I replied, "Sir, I am sorry, I don't want to copy any answer. Please, don't inform the proctor about this. I am sorry sir," I started weeping in a deserted class. "Shhhh.......Shhhhh.......relax, relax, calm down! This is a favour I am extending to you", whispered Ravinder. "Favour?" I said with a blank face. "Just copy it down hurry," Ravinder chattered.

I didn't give it a second thought and jotted all the answers in the blink of an eye. I submitted the answer sheet to Ravinder with a frightened look on the face. Dots of sweat were popping up and condensing all over my face. I picked up my bag and sprinted. Called mom but couldn't reach her. I wanted to share this with somebody, but alas I had none. I walked till the last mile of the college campus and tears started rolling down my cheeks in melancholy. It was a breezy day, but that breeze couldn't touch my wounds to ease the agony. My face was covered by hands, sieving my tears, tickling on my dress. And, suddenly a voice said, "Pooja?" The voice sounded hopeful, enthralling me to look up. It was the Ravinder again. "Why are you weeping, my doll? Did I say anything to offend you or did I misbehave with you? Please forgive me if I did so. Come, let's go for a ride on my bike. It will lift your mood". I knew he was hoodwinking me into something which really interests him, but with an addlepated mind, I replied, "No, I am alright. Just guilty of connivance."Ravinder replied, "Connivance? Really? Come on, you didn't do anything wrong. It was the entire class, and what was the option you were left with? So cheer up. I will take you for a ride and drop you back to your hostel."

I nodded in denial and stood up. I started walking towards my hostel. Perplexed Ravinder, started following me dauntlessly, screaming, "Pooja, let's go. Where are you going? If you don't stop at once, I will inform the dean that you copied the answers in your lab assessment." My scudding movements suddenly came to a still down, and a deep silence prevailed. I started shivering in the consternation of being caught. Ravinder covered the gap and ran close to me, creating a vacuum between his and my face. "So, will you now accept the offer of riding with me?" I dropped my eyelids like a poor little thing and spoke in agreement, "Ok! I will ride on your bike, but you got to promise me that you won't threaten me further. This chapter closes today with this bike ride". Ravinder exclaimed, "Bravo! Good Girl. Come on, sit up and hold me tight, because this is college campus and even the walls got eyes." I uncomfortably sat behind him on his bike, holding the back support, while he rode it in posthaste.

"Pooja, Pooja, Are you there?" questioned Ravinder. I, with a sad face, was lost in a small battle with myself wondering if I have done the right thing by agreeing with him or not. I knew I didn't, and it could cause severe consequences for that. For the next 30 minutes, we were mute. All I could hear was the rattling tires with a gust of wind. My inertia of motion came to rest suddenly, and I stumbled upon Ravinder carelessly. He turned his head towards me with a devious grin. I collected myself in hesitation and apologised to him, "I am sorry, the brakes were too hard to control. I lost my balance." Ravinder smiled and said, "I would love to have such imbalances quite often." Pooja shivered in fear. "Where are we now? You told me that we were going for a stroll around the campus, but the signboards around tell a different story. Let's get back to the University. It's already quarter to five. I have to be in the hostel by 6:30 PM. Ravinder with his ugly, dirty teeth, smiled again and said, "Let's get ourselves comfortable at my friend's guest house. We will soon leave for the campus." Ravinder, at that time, appeared to me as the progenitor of the character 'Ravana from The Ramayana. I felt like I have been abducted. Waiting for him at a dirty restaurant, daunting thoughts were running through my mind. I wanted to run but don't know what was stopping me. I closed my eyes and started praying to God to help me to escape from this situation. Standing alone, waiting, unable to remonstrate against the happenings, I was importuning God, "Shiva, please help me. Lord Shiva, please save me."

When a hand rested on my shoulder, I jerked it in extreme fear of being molested. I shouted and screamed, "Ah.........Ah.........."I heard a voice, trying to comfort me. "Pooja, Pooja, Pooja, relax Pooja, it's me Sachin. Pooja. I am from your college. I am in the Mechanical branch. Pooja, it's Sachin".

I busted into tears and hugged Sachin, begging him to take me out of this place. I cried, "Please, take me out of this place. Please save me. Please guide me out of this place". Sachin understood that there was something fishy going on. He helped me to the nearest auto and booked it for the university. I kept my eyes closed, resting my head on his shoulder. Sachin's brave gestures were very comforting, and I felt that I could trust him.. We reached college in exactly thirty minutes. Sachin dropped me at the hostel without asking a single question, and I didn't utter a word too. That evening, I received two hundred missed calls from that rascal Ravinder. I didn't pick any of them nor did I revert to any of his messages.

I was lying on my single bed, clutching my pillow and thanking Sachin restlessly for saving me. If Sachin hadn't come to my rescue, I would have been doomed today. Two of my neighbours knocked on my door, but I didn't respond. I picked up my laptop to search for Sachin's name in the mechanical department directory. "Ok, Google, URL: https://delhiengineeringcollege.in/student_directoty/mechanical_department.

"There he is— Sachin Rathore ," I exclaimed in joy. 'My hero of the day. I should meet him and thank him for his help. I shall finish off the classes tomorrow and see him by the end of the day,' I promised to myself.

Another bright day and I hurriedly had my breakfast and ran for my computer lab exam. The entire day was a dime a dozen. But I was waiting for my special evening. The day passed by, and I was on the ball. The computer lab was adjacent to the electronics lab. I was quite vexed with what had happened yesterday and didn't want to see that bastard's face again. I bit the bullet and submitted my answer sheet, at last, but found that I was the last person in the exam hall. I twisted my wrist, "Oh my God, it's already five-ten. I should rush. Sachin will leave for his hostel," I reminded myself. I was bolting out when I crashed on Ravinder. I de-accelerated my speed and tried to pull myself together.

We were face to face at the exit of the computer lab. Ravinder raised his finger towards me, saying, "You left me yesterday. Now you just wait and watch what I do to you." I was getting bent out of shape for what he said, but Sachin was still on my mind. I collected my bag and ran towards the Mechanical department, panting and struggling for breath. I stopped halfway after I saw Sachin coming towards me. Sachin said, "Hey, Pooja, I was coming to see you and break the ice." I was panting, but still smiling. We shook hands and walked to the nearest cafe.

"So, will you now, please, throw some light on what had happened yesterday?" questioned Sachin.

I replied, "Just one small help cost me an arm and a leg."

"Please, Pooja, I have been so restless about your condition last evening. Please, entail the details. I am running out of patience," jeered Sachin.

Pooja replied, "We will cross the bridge once we come across it. I wanted to thank you for yesterday's selfless help. I know I misbehaved and I am apologising for that."Sachin held my hand and said, "Please don't cut around the corners and don't make a long story short. Go back to the drawing board and tell me how did it all happen? You were in the fustiest place in Delhi. As far as I know you, you are the university topper and extremely talented girl. I was wondering what could have compelled you to visit such a place?"

Tears welled up in my eyes, slowly trickling down my cheeks. Sachin comforted me, saying, "Hang in there. Let yourself off the hook. You can tell me what had happened and I assure you I won't judge you."

I started, "I was wrapping my head around the electronics question paper when I realised the entire class was talking that 99% of the article was out of syllabus. A notorious kid happened to find all the answers from the book, and the whole level copied the answers, except me. Nobody bothered to pass on the sheet to me. I was struggling through the perfect storm when Ravinder came to my rescue with the cheat answer sheet. But, he offered a deal to me where he asked me return the favour to him when required. I didn't give it a second thought and agreed to what he said, in fear of failing by the skin of my teeth.".

I was sobbing. Sachin patted my back, saying, "Every cloud has a silver lining. I will fix this for you. You give Ravinder the cold shoulder, and we will handle him now. Let's get going. It's going to be six-thirty, time for your hostel gate closure".

We walked to the hostel again, and he bid me goodnight. I entered the gate thinking about him. I knew I have started liking him, but just as a friend. "Oh, I forgot to take his number," I uttered and ran towards the gate but Sachin was gone. 'Never mind, some other day maybe', I smiled and felt happy for the first time in the last three years for being friends with someone, who is selfless and caring. But maybe I should take it with a pinch of salt. I was scared if someday he would also turn out to be like other men. I jerked away from these aberrant thoughts.

'Woah, mom is calling. What a happy day!'

"Hi mom, how are you? How is it going? I met a friend today, Sachin. Just a nice guy, mom," the happy blabber continued for hours. The day ended on a good note. I am a rising star amongst girls now, not for my academics but for my next affair. I often overheard girls saying, "She ditched Jai and now she is after poor Sachin. She is such a virus which can deactivate anybody's system." The jealousy and cynicism made its ways to my ears but they soon turned futile as exams were near. Exams had made students sit on the fence. Papers were too tough to answer.

While I was shaping up my answer sheets, Sachin was shipping out his exams, knocking Ravinder with some of the seniors of our college. Things were going out of the frying pan to the fire for Ravinder.

Every day, five students would invade the electronics lab and punch him for his deeds. Ravinder would plead for mercy, but no one cared. After all, the students were getting a chance to fist their energies.

Our exams were scheduled in a way that they would end in a week and a half. I appeared in all my tests and did exceptionally well. Sachin, too, appeared in all the exams but finished them in just 45 minutes to utilise the rest of his time in testing Ravinder's bearing capacity. On the last day of the review, students jumped on the bandwagon to beat Ravinder. Sachin made sure that the news wouldn't spread like a wildfire. Nobody spoke about it amongst their friends or in the college management. Ravinder finally agreed to make an apology to me on the day when every student had left for home.

On the last day of the exam, exhilarated Sachin ran to my examination room. He was watching me from the window. I was binding my answer sheets in great contentment. He didn't speak a word but waited for me patiently till the time I reached my bag for stowing my belongings.

"Hey, Pooja. How are you? How was the exam," Sachin questioned aloud.

I turned and cried in joy, "Hi, Sachin. The exam went superfluously well. How are you? How was your exam?"

"They were super. I got some good news for you," said Sachin.

"Oh! Really? What is it? Are you scoring 99 out of 100 in Maths this time? I know you are an outstanding Mathematician. A lot of girls in my hostel keep on telling me," I replied.

"No way! Girls talking about me in the hostel? Shhh, seems like my lucky days are around. The good news is that Ravinder is ready to apologise to you for his mistake. Sorry, not a mistake but a heinous crime. I made sure he learnt a lesson, and he won't do this to anyone ever now."

"What? I mean...How? What did you do? And my marks for the lab?" I uttered nervously.

"It is a snowball effect. Our seniors helped me to bring him down. We made sure he doesn't complain to the college administration for this. You have successfully secured an excellent grade, and he is coming to apologise tomorrow early morning," comforted Sachin.

"Thank you so much, Sachin. I don't know how to thank you for helping me in turning a storm into a tea-cup. You are a true friend. Let's grab an ice cream: after all, it's time for celebrations. The treat is on me," I said happily.

Sachin smiled and scratched his head with a shy smile. "Ok, if you say so."

We wended off the roads, talking, teasing and laughing while getting our celebratory ice cream scoops. He made his choice at the ice-cream parlour, and I juggled my wallet to check for sixty rupees. I handed over the change to Sachin, asking him to pay the ice-cream vendor, while I was keeping my wallet in my purse. "Oh, it's done. Let's go", said Sachin. I raised my head and replied, "Yeah, let's go."

CHAPTER 4
RISE OF EMOTIONS

Sachin dropped me off to my hostel once again today, but this time, with a gesture that I couldn't understand. He renamed me P. Rathore.

"From today, I will call you P. Rath. Ok?" said Sachin.

"Why?" I raised my eyebrow.

Sachin replied, "Because you are my friend now. Friendship gives me all the reasons to keep both of us happy."

I nodded my head in agreement and entered the hostel. There were butterflies in my stomach, and I was on cloud nine. Well begun is half done in friendship. I think it is going to last long. I don't want to lose him at any cost. I am apprehended in my decision of being with him for the lifetime. The best thing about him is that I had known him for two weeks now, but he never asked for my number. Strange! Isn't it? He is a sober boy. The girl who gets married to him will be the luckiest. That evening was spent in packing up the bags for departure on the next day. I was leaving for home for the first time during my college tenure. As always, I didn't want to go. I wanted to spend more time with Sachin, embracing our friendship. I was confused if I should be conveying my emotions to Sachin or not. The night turned into a rhyme, and I jotted my first literary contemplation on bonding with a stranger. It read:I don't dream of a charming prince,

Just one, who is made of love centuries since,

Sparkling eyes drenched in passion,

Someone, whose honesty never goes out of fashion.

It feels like a sweet confusion,

Coz I just see him in a mirror of illusion.

I don't dream of a multimillionaire,

Just one who has learnt to care,

Crystal touch and those warm hands,

Someone, who takes me to fairylands.

It feels like a sweet confusion,

Coz it is a question with no solution.

I don't dream of a dashing handsome,

Just one whose heart is a king's ransom,

Luscious lips surrounded by the groomed beard,

As if God himself has appeared.

It feels like a sweet confusion,

Coz it's nothing more than self-delusion.

I don't dream of muscular Hercules,

Just one who is sweetest to be chased by killer bees,

A rock chest throned like Mother's lap,

Someone who could make me smile in a snap.

It feels like a sweet confusion,

Coz, such thoughts are silent seclusion.

I don't dream of my dream man,

That I did never, no, nor never can,

An imagination so supreme,

Someone shall never dare to dream,

It feels like a sweet confusion,

Coz my dreams died in his illusion.

I woke up from my dreams the next morning, all set with my luggage. Right outside my hostel, Ravinder was standing with five seniors from my department. As I exited the hostel gate, my keen eyes were searching for Sachin. I walked closer to Ravinder, when a voice from behind rejoiced me. "P. Rath. Here I am? I was right beside you, and you didn't see me.".I was laconic in my response. I just smiled and said, "Oops........ I am sorry." Ravinder was begging me to forgive him. I uttered, "The most effective way of punishing him is to not to speak a word. You are an unscrupulous teacher. I won't forgive you ever. Albeit, you can continue teaching here, if you follow the rules and regulations." One of the seniors said, "Don't worry Pooja, we will keep an eye on him." I replied, "Thank you, sir." I bade bye to all the seniors, while Sachin accompanied me to the main gate.

"So, what's the plan at home? You are going home. I will miss you here," said Sachin.

"Why? Aren't you going home?" I questioned.

"Hahaha... Yes, I am going home too, but tomorrow. Your auto is here. Take your seat and do let me know if you feel things are dicy," advised Sachin.

"But how? I don't have your number." I questioned.

"Oh yeah! There you go. Could you just hold my wallet and take out a card there? My details are mentioned there. I have to take this urgent call."I nodded in agreement. I opened up the wallet and found the same sixty rupee notes in the wallet with *P. Rath* written over it. I was baffled but tried to hide it by picking a card from the strip. After a second of speculation, I asked Sachin, "Are these the same notes that I gave for the ice-cream party?"

Sachin replied, "Yes. **P. Rath** everything given by you is essential to me. If you think this isn't right, I shall return these back to you. My grandmother used to tell me, never let go of the things you embrace in your life. For me, your friendship is valuable, and every single bit of it matters."

There were tears in his eyes. I said, "I am so lucky to have you."

I got out of the auto and hugged him. This was the biggest moment of my life. The journey from the hostel back to home felt like a beautiful walk. I am sure there is a method to his madness. I know the devil is in detail; still, I like this boy very much. I am surely gonna miss him a lot for one month. I reached the airport, picked out his card from my bag and texted him for the first time. The text read, 'Thank you so much. I will miss you'. The time at the airport passed while waiting for his reply. Ten minutes later, my phone buzzed. No, it wasn't him. Every time I looked at the phone felt like a wild goose chase. I have boarded the flight and about to take off. The phone buzzed again, "I will miss you too my P. Rath. Sorry for the late reply, but you should have dropped your name at the end of the message, you silly," read the text from Sachin. I was filled with exultation while hovering in the skies.

Back home, the two months long vacation was not coming to an end. Every other day felt like a dreary day. I was at home but was missing college. Wait... What? College? No way, nothing is riveting in there. I was missing someone else. I was friends with someone for the first time in the last three years. Fifteen days had already passed, and I was all alone at home. Mom and dad were out on an office tour. I was lying on my bed, checking my emails, when a message came from an anonymous source, "Hey, How are you?" At first, I thought it would be Sachin. I jumped out of my bed and unlocked my screen to open the message. I replied, "Hey Sachin. How are you doing?" I was eagerly waiting for him to reply. Five minutes passed and yet, no reply. Now, I am walking to and forth, waiting for his response. Half an hour passed but no response. I am going to the kitchen to cook something for myself.

The phone buzzed and I ran back to the phone kept on my study table. ''Finally, the message arrived', I rejoiced in excitement. The message read, "Hey Pooja, Rahul this side. How are you doing? Let's catch up" I was surprised after reading this. This was Rahul, whom I knew in my school days. I replied, "Oh yes! Rahul from St. Mary's School?" My text was followed by Rahul's writing, "Yes, you recognised me. I saw your picture on Facebook. You have grown up to be an angel". I ignored his word, for I was cherishing my new friendship with Sachin.

CHAPTER-5
THE DRASTIC U-TURN

Finally, the vacations were over, and I was returning to Delhi via train. The eagerness to meet Sachin was at the peak. On platform No. 2, every other person looked like Sachin to me. I would turn around every time to check if the person is actually Sachin, or was it merely infatuation.

I smiled and blushed at this stupidity of mine. The train was a little delayed, and I was as always ahead of time. My loneliness had all the reasons to show me my stature. At the end of the vacations, lots of parents came down to the station to bid adieu to their children. Siblings were playing around, teasing each other and making plans for the next meeting while I was sitting alone at the station, only accompanied by my statutory imaginations. The clock struck 4. My train was scheduled to depart from Delhi railway station at 1:30 pm. "What a shame is this railway system?" I exclaimed with a yawn. With a list long of luggage, I relaxed on the platform's floors, as the announcement said, "The announcement for the arrival of Kirti Express, plying between Varanasi and Delhi will be made soon. We apologize for the inconvenience caused to our passengers." I smiled and took out my diary from my purse. If not people, at least words will help me bite this bullet of predicament of railways. I was wondering what I should write about when suddenly, the evergreen thought of Sachin popped up in my mind, and I started-

I am here,

Still waiting for you,

The routes to reach you are suspended,

But, my wait for you never ended.

I am still here,

Listening to your favourite song,

The silence in the town has descended,

But my wait for you never ended.

I am still here,

Remembering the worst of our fights,

The worse to correct is all extended,

But my wait for you never ended.

I am still here,

Hearing your blissful soft rebukes,

Nothing uttered, yet all comprehended,

But my wait for you never ended.

I am still here,

Making silly mistakes to seek your cover,

That by no means has been amended,

But my wait for you never ended.

I will always be here,

Even if, I tear down,

And that my dust was to the earth commended,

Only your kiss shall have my wait ended.

In the rush of thoughts, I didn't realize how it was 1:00 am
at night. Writing is such a magical getaway for me. It eats
away all the problems. Boozing will always be my second

priority if pen and paper are with me. Finally, I boarded the train, occupied my seat and dropped a message to my mother that I have safely boarded the train. In the second class compartment, I was the only girl. Quite astonishing, but that might explain why India needs slogans like 'Beti Bacho, Beto Padhao' (save the girl child, educate the girl child). Indians need to be conscious about gender discrimination.

"I am eagerly waiting for the sun to rise and shine, abolishing such cruel mindset against girls and set me free first. Hehehe, it's good to be selfish sometimes. Isn't it?" I engaged myself in a monologue while waiting in a queue for beddings. Two-way traffic was enough to create commotion in the narrow alley. The hue and cry for something which you have already paid for was quite annoying. Still, I maintained my patience until this guy, coming from the opposite direction, lost his balance and fell over me. "I am so sorry, ma'am, I just can't control this ambush. Are you hurt?" apologised the healthy boy. "First, get off me," I cried in anger. He lifted himself with a great effort, leaving me flat gasping for breath. It felt as if I was churned by a wheel loader. For five minutes, I had an out-of-body experience. I had barely opened my eyes when a voice echoed around, "Hey! Pooja. What a coincidence, man. You are on the same train". The view was blurred. All I could remember were three gentle ladies helping me to get on my feet, and a happy face saying, "I am Rahul. Are you ok? Your classmate, Rahul". I restored all my energy and replied, "Whoever you are, please help me back to my seat". He replied, "Sure. Why don't you take my seat?" I scoffed angrily, "5C is the number I am travelling on. If you can't help me, let me ask somebody else". Rahul's idiocy was irritating me. My seat was on the far end of the boogie, and I took some 8 minutes limping to get back to my place. I sat on my chair and expressed my wish to lie down. Rahul, within no time, helped me to grab a pillow, placed it below my head and sat next to my legs on the same berth. I slept for an hour and woke up in agitation when I heard someone reciting my recent poem. It was Rahul, reading out my diary.

"How dare you through my stuff?" I shouted drawing everyone's attention.

"I just appreciated your writing skills, Pooja," explained Rahul.

"Will you please, get back to your seat? Thank you so much for all your help. But, I want some time alone," I said.

Rahul left the berth and walked out of the boogie.

The journey was of nearly 14 hours. I just wanted to reach Delhi as soon as possible. I texted Sachin, "Boarded the train and met with an accident. Worry not! I am fine. Hope to see you at 2:00 PM at Old Delhi railway station. The train is arriving at platform No. 4. Please, enquire for the correct platform No. in case there are some last-minute changes." The cell-phone is such a magnet. It keeps me attached until I receive a response from Sachin. Checking phone every five minutes is exasperating most of the times. I got up in restlessness as he hadn't replied. Never had I ever got so much attention from someone like him. He had somehow become very special for me. I was sure that he was my best friend. I gathered my slippers to go to the washroom. I had just crossed two berths when my phone rang. I rushed back, anticipating Sachin's call in response. I picked the call without even reading out the name. "Hey, Sachin I am on the train," I spoke enliveningly. "Uhh… Pooja, it's me, Rahul. I am just a boogie away. In case you want me to get something to eat for you, don't hesitate to call. Please, save my number," Rahul spoke softly. I apologised, "Sorry Rahul, I didn't know it was you". "It's okay, never mind. Call me," spoke Rahul and hung up.

Just after the call, Rahul banged into the boogie, saying, "I thought you must be in pain." I understood he is planning to spend the night with me on my berth. I said, "Alright, I am also not very sleepy, let's talk." Rahul smiled and sat close to my foot. The conversation started with, "You remember, I used to sit right next to you in class, and you never noticed?" I giggled and replied, "Oh, yes. I barely remember you, Rahul. Those days, oh my God!" The talks went for a while till both of us passed out. It was from 2:00 PM. Both of us were buried into each other, sleeping carelessly. The train was about to reach the station. People were gathering their belongings, and we were sleeping as if we don't belong to this planet any more. My phone was ringing. Sachin had called 27 times and left 72 messages. The train applied the brakes and the Old Delhi station, platform no. 4, welcomed its tired passengers. I was still sleeping and so was Rahul. Nobody was kind enough to make an effort to wake us up.

Slowly all the passengers descended the train. Sachin entered boogie no. 2A. He looked tensed and started searching for me everywhere in the compartment. Finally, he found me sleeping in Rahul's lap.

CHAPTER 6
THE AGONISTIC BEGINNING

"Pooja, Pooja, Pooja........." Sachin shouted, hitting Rahul. "Get off her. How dare you touch her? Pooja, what did he do with you? Did he sedate you? I will drag him to women's cell. This rascal has to pay for that. You come here and stay behind me. I will kill this bastard."I pleaded iteratively, "Sachin, please, leave him. He is a friend from school. Don't hit him. We accidentally slept together. Not together, I mean we were just talking, and I don't know what to say."Sachin was hitting Rahul aggressively and Rahul was begging Sachin to stop. He cried, "I didn't do anything. Why are you beating me mercilessly? Pooja is with me on her own will. I love her, and she loves me. Who are you to say anything?"

I shouted, "Rahul, are you insane? When did I say that I love you? I barely know you. Sachin, don't listen to him." I started hitting Rahul too. But a couple of seconds later, Sachin stopped and disembarked the train. Rahul ran for his life, leaving me all alone there. I grabbed my luggage and stepped out of the boogie. Sachin was standing with drooping shoulders, holding his head in his hand. I walked closer to him and tried to talk to him amidst the screeching engine noise. He didn't hear me. I walked closer this time, very close to his ear and shouted, "Sachin, I am sorry for such trenchant scene. The severity of the situation is uncompromising, but you have to trust me." Sachin didn't utter a word. He lifted my bags, and we hired an auto for the college. His silence was indicative of a storm.

Something was not right. I tried to talk to Sachin, but all in vain. He paid the auto driver and asked him to drop me off to the girls' hostel. No replies to any of my questions. I understood that Sachin has misinterpreted the entire situation. I wanted to say sorry. It was just like a storm in a teacup. Sachin was nowhere in college. I checked for him in the library, in his class, and in his hostel room. He just vanished. My aspirations to spend time with him went down in flames. Days passed, months passed and finally, the semester exams approached for the final year. The classrooms of 60 students looked vacant in every lecture. Every name starting with 'S' seemed like it was spelt for Sachin. Eyes were waiting for him. My ears wanted to hear him. Heartbeat would slow down whenever my phone rang. I was obsessed with him. My smile had shrunk to a straight sealed silence.

Maybe, I was counting my chicken before they hatched. The final exams were tough this time, and I was the jack of all trades, for the only thing I did this semester was to study in agony. I stayed back in the hostel after semester end. Hovering around the hostel like a dreadful soul in evocation of those legendary moments of my life.

The break was of 15 days. I counted my days, not from the last day of the exams, but from the date I last saw Sachin. Every second of the day was dedicated to him, and every string of thought wept in his separation, which read as:Born all nude,

My soul between the kisses and wine,

High on unlimited attitude,

My sufferings were enclosed in a crystal shrine.

Crawling floors and climbing laps,

Father felt magic and mother felt divine,

Happiness inside always snaps,

My sufferings were pleasures fair and fine.

The world slowly expanded,

New features, accent and thoughts would come to me incline,

Meeting people and my wish was commanded,

My sufferings now started making a vigorous line.

My collar all high and grown,

Life is in haste, every task willing to resign,

Hiding and weeping on roads, alone,

My sufferings every time appeared in a new design.

Looking for shoulder and shelter,

All, my heart and mind, in search of a happy sign,

No way out to escape this boiling swelter,

Had I known, my sufferings are just mine.

The long wait of aspiring students was finally over. It was the result day, and the five best companies, including TCL, Y Comm. Ltd., Hygiene Delve were conducting their rounds of interviews based on the results. Different companies had different cut-offs. For the branch toppers, getting a job was like icing on the cake. They were welcoming toppers readily and offered them the topmost packages of the industry. I was sitting right outside the classroom corridor, and students congratulating me on my record-breaking performance this semester. "Hey, Pooja. Congrats! You are the gold medalist and topper of all the branches. I knew you would do it. I am proud of you," an anonymous voice waved around my ears from behind.

Tears rolled down my cheeks, touching my lips, which murmured Sachin. With my eyes closed, stretching the straight sealed lips to make the best "U", I ran towards the voice with my eyes closed and hugged him tightly. "Where were you, I missed you badly?" I whispered. He whispered in my ears, "Just a second Pooja, please look at me." I denied to leave him and wanted to put my arms around him till eternity. I realised that he wasn't holding me. Something seemed incomplete. I stepped back. Opened my eyes and saw his hand tightly clutched with the palm of another young, fair lady. She was wearing a Sindoor (a vermillion powder, often seen as a symbol of marriage) and red-coloured bangles till the elbow. I stepped back with an intense look. "Sachhinnn...... When did this happen? You got married?" I asked in a traumatized manner. "Isn't she beautiful? Her name is Tara. We got married 2 months back, and I left college. Joined dad's business and we honeymooned in Thailand last month," narrated Sachin while Tara smiled in excitement. "Wow, wow, wow, I am so happy for you," I just spoke and paused. "Anyways catch you around. TCL has hired you already. Your name is on the list. Go and check out. They are looking for you all around for the HR round. I thought I should meet you and congratulate you in person," announced Sachin.

He walked away with a smiling face and painful eyes. I could see the unforgiveness in his eyes. Tara, utterly unaware of our eye-to-eye conversation, hugged me and bade goodbye.

That day, action spoke louder than words. His marriage was an insult added to my injury. Not that I wanted to marry him, but I knew that I had lost the only best friend I had. I would never get a chance to explain, and he would live his life with hatred against me. The only alternative was to move on, walk away from the memories, and try to establish a new presence in a new city. Indeed, the girl who got married to him is the luckiest. I nodded in agreement and accepted my first job offer letter at TCL.

CHAPTER 7
THINK, WORK, SLEEP, REPEAT

My first day in the office was right after the semester result. Fortunately, I was posted in the Delhi office of TCL. No high heels, no short skirts and no fancy handbags, I dressed up in suit-salwar with flats, a carry bag with a heavy laptop, handed over to me in the college itself and a small bindi on the forehead. I had no reasons to celebrate. The guilt of not being able to explain myself lived inside me like a perfect storm, which never allowed me to be happy and enjoy the things around me. The big dreams of a small town-girl were smashed into pieces when I entered the office. The position of the reception seemed very practical, not like the Bollywood offices, where the receptionists didn't even care if you have registered the punch or not. No morning wishes or hellos. People looked more like slaves than employees. The Matrix philosophy proved increasingly germane when I checked out the office ambience. "My reporting is to Mr. Jeeva Kanyal. Could you please assist me to his chamber?" I asked the receptionist politely. She stared at me and spoke rudely, "Do you have his phone number? If yes, please, help yourself by calling him and if not, try calling your HR, who can help you with his number." I grumbled, "I am new to this place and today is my first day. Is this the way you behave with the new employees?" She ignored me to the height and walked away to the washroom. "What the f.....?" I whispered.. I searched for my phone and started walking briskly to the exit. My eyes were fixed on the phone. Bang! His shoulder rubbed against mine, and I shouted, "Ouchh...."

"Sorry, sorry. Are you ok?" the man replied.

I looked at him and spoke, "I am sorry, maybe it was my mistake. I am seeking help, but none seems to help me, Mr......"

I searched for his name on his hanging identity card. "Mr. Jeeva Kalyan," he replied.

"Oh...Oh.   Good...Good...Mornin...Morning,   sir," I fumbled.

"I am Pooja, from Delhi College. I was shortlisted to work under you in the R&D department. I was searching for you, but this receptionist…." I was explaining when I got interrupted by him.

"No worries, Pooja. Welcome to the team. We finally meet. I have heard about your remarkable performance in college. We are glad to have you on board. We look forward to utilising your skills for the betterment of the company. Please, follow me to your workplace. I shall introduce you to your colleagues," said Mr. Jeeva.

I just readily followed Him. 'New girl in the office. Hey, new girl,' the whispers were quite annoying. It felt like I am the newly wedded bride in the village and people were queuing up to catch a glimpse of me. I thought that I was no Miss Universe or a beauty pageant queen yet, people were gawking at me. I felt so uncomfortable. Never mind, just kept walking with my eyes straight and head down.

"Hi, Sudarshan. She is Pooja, our new R&D engineer. She is a gold medalist from Delhi College. She passed this year. Our company selected her through the on-campus process. Over to you now. Explain the job details and the work profile to her," Mr. Jeeva advised Sudarshan, my new team lead. Sudarshan shook hands with Jeeva and the latter retired to his chamber. "Miss Pooja, welcome to the TCL R&D department. This is our workspace," Sudarshan spoke, giving a welcoming gesture. Sudarshan took me to the cubicle and introduced me to the entire team— Mannu,

Sakshi, Rakhi, Jai, Ajit, Vallabh, and Arijit. Everyone shook hands and congratulated me on the new role. The office was average. Everyone had a separate cubicle, and my working lounge was right in front of Mr. Jeeva's. Never mind, the first day was a mere introduction with the office mates and the ambience. I had a single week-off only on Sunday. Interacting with new colleagues and knowing the rules and regulations was pretty exciting during the first week.

My lodging was in one of the nearest PGs, which constituted of working professionals of all kinds. This was a women's PG and was located at some 45 minutes distance from the office. The early working days were very hectic. I would dream of escalations and emergencies every night during my intern stage because the penalties were high on missing some alarms as they affect the system on a bigger scale, imposing massive sanctions on TCL. Mr. Jeeva was stringent, and his loud howling on any mistakes would scare the hell out of me. Entire team's track record was good because of the way Mr. Jeeva used to get the tasks executed in the organization. Mr. Jeeva was around 42-years old, smart, tall and good looking. He was passionate and penchant about his work. He was the best-dressed gentleman in the entire office. Arijit was the most friendly, facetious and helping colleague in my team. He would accompany me to the office cafes for lunch and evening tea. He would even drop me to the taxi stand. Our friendship was gradually growing strong. But I often missed Sachin. His sense of humour was obnoxiously intoxicating. Arijit stood close to Sachin, but Sachin's place was irreplaceable. The work at the office was growing exponentially frantic. Staying late at offices was now a regular trait for the R&D department. Since I used to put up in PG, I was least worried about rushing home. Still, being a creative writer, I always felt the craving for little time to pen down my emotions. Mr. Jeeva looked happy and even a little curious about my visits to the client locations. He had been enquiring about my punch-in and punch-out timings. The other day, Sakshi mentioned during the lunch hour, "Jeeva sir was asking about your card punching time. I said Pooja reached office sharp at 9:00 am. The client is happy with her designs and solutions." I freckled, worried if I have done something wrong because Jeeva sir barely intervenes in employee timesheets and punches. My subconscious mind was on high alert. It compelled me to be very punctual in reaching office as well as the client location on dot time.

Although he never mentioned this to me in the last three months, my job could be in danger. Keeping this in mind, I entered the office at 9:00 pm for some breakout emergency. This time, I was on night shift for the first time and I again bumped into him. Who? Mr. Jeeva! He was still in the office.

"Pooja, why are you here at this time?" questioned Jeeva sir.

I replied, "Sir, actually there was an emergency. I had to come to the office as everyone is on leave for Diwali. So..."

"But, why didn't you go for Diwali celebrations?" a curious question by Mr. Jeeva.

"Well, I didn't feel like going. My mom is on tour, and I am not very close to my dad," I spoke with little watery eyes, followed by a long pause.

"I see. Leave all this work, let go out today for celebrations," insisted Mr. Jeeva.

"No, sir, the client is dropping aggressive emails. I have to address this issue. Thank you, but maybe some other time. That's very kind of you," I replied hesitantly.

"Hmm…. as you wish, I won't force you, but I can call for a substitute if you change your mind," proposed Mr. Jeeva.

"No, sir, I am fine. Thank you," I answered politely.

He smiled and patted my back while opening the exit door. I took small steps ahead, and we crossed each other after a short conversation. That night was way more hectic than I had expected. At one point, I was cursing myself for denying Mr. Jeeva's proposal. "Huh, what a bad night it is. The problem doesn't seem to get solved," I murmured. "There is nothing which can't be solved. You are over-stressing. The traffic has improved over the server. Thanks to your hard work," a voice echoed from behind. I turned back but found nobody. Amazeballs were ringing around. Unexpectedly, a hand approached towards me from the right side, and I gasped for a breath.

"You scared the hell out of me!" I screamed.

He laughed saying, "That's my style of introducing myself to nerds and brainiacs. I am Shahid." "It's the most vacuous way of self-introduction I have ever come across," I frowned and replied.

"Cheer up. I apologise for this prank. I have been a massive fan of your problem-solving approach and methodologies. The way you are achieving milestones in R&D, you will soon end up being the CEO of TCL," Shahid praised.

I coughed and continued, "Stop making mole out of a hill. How can I help you?" "Straight on point. Very professional," confessed Shahid.

"Yes, and if it is nothing, allow me some time. I have to urgently make a call," I made an escaping excuse and walked towards the floor gallery. Acting intentionally as if was actually making a call, I walked out of his sight and peeped out of the gallery. To my astonishment, I found Mr. Jeeva sitting right outside the reception. I wondered what he was waiting for. Must be work!. I walked inside and completed the rest of my work for the night. I was so damn sleepy but somehow, managed to walk. I was about to step into the muddy pit but slipped into someone's firm arms.

I almost lost my balance and thought that would get considerably hurt this time. Nevertheless, somebody saved me. Who? It was Mr. Jeeva.

"Sir, you? How come? You left at 9:30 PM then how are you here early morning?" I questioned while he was holding me firmly in his arms.

He replied, "Yeah, had to come to the office early morning. Perhaps, God is kind on you. And fortunately, I was passing by."

"Uh... yeah. Thank you so much, sir. Have a nice day, sir" I said while lifting myself and walked towards the taxi stand.

CHAPTER 8
THE FIRST KISS

In a pell-mell, I boarded the office shuttle, stowed my bag in the luggage cabin and secured my seat. "Phew, what a long night it was," I said while stretching. The seat right next to me was vacant. I was praying for it to stay vacant for next 1 hour at least. But, God is not always kind. Guess what? Who came to share the journey with me? I literally closed my eyes and covered my face with my hands to escape this torture. Ignorant of my plea to God, he sat right next to me. I avoided him as long as I could. He took no time in identifying me and said, "Hey, miss brainy. How are you doing?" It was Shahid again. I didn't reply, acting as if I was sleeping. He intruded once more, "Excuse me, Are you listening to me?" I appeared dead, without even moving a single cell of my body, speaking metaphorically. Shahid reclined his seat as per his comfort. This was the most dreadful travel back home. His presence was keeping me on my toes. I just didn't want to open up my eyes and indulge in lame conversation with him. I almost dropped out in sleep. My siesta was too engaging, making me travel to a different world entirely. I could clearly see Mr. Jeeva, Shahid and I standing in a room with the most provoked looks. Shahid advanced closer to me, grabbed my waist, pulled me towards him, holding onto my hair and started to undress my lips with his. The smooch had just started when a hard jerk left Shahid and I wide-eye opened, holding onto each other's breaths. I could see Shahid bleeding, and he fell down with open eyes. I fell following him while Mr Jeeva held a blood-red knife, grinning over our dead bodies. I screamed in the bus, holding Shahid tightly. The driver stopped the bus by applying hydraulic brakes. The co-passengers ran towards the scream to check for the occurrence. I was panting and sweating badly. Shahid handled the situation saying, "She is absolutely ok. It was just a bad dream. I will take care of her. Please, drop us here. I will take her on a walk." Shahid put his arms around me and carefully walked behind me, helping me disembark the bus. He patted on the bus, signalling the driver to take it onward. The bus left. Shahid booked a cab to my home destination. It was still 15 minutes from that point while I was sitting on a chair at a bus stand with the most horrified looks. Shahid was mature enough not to plunge into questionnaires. On the spur of the moment, a car stopped with the most screeching brakes. I was hoping this to be our ride home. "Pooja, let's go home," the voice appeared to be distant. I lifted my face up and was amazed to find Mr. Jeeva in his car, honking and shouting, "Pooja, let's go home." I turned left to look for Shahid. He was still busy booking the cab, unaware of Mr. Jeeva's presence. Mr. Jeeva stepped out of his car and came across me. "Why aren't you listening to me? I will drop you home. Cabs are limited today," he spoke in concern. I walked towards Shahid hurriedly uttering, "Mr. Jeeva is here for us. Perhaps he will drop us home." Shahid gave me a thunderbolt look, without uttering a word. Shahid walked with me towards his car, helping me to get inside. Shahid was about to hop in the car when Jeeva sir interrupted by coughing and said, "Why don't you take the next bus. I have to pick my family on the way. Since this is a 5-seater, everyone won't be able to adjust." Shahid, with one foot inside the car glanced at me. "Alright sir, I am sure you can drop Pooja well on time. I shall take the next bus," saying this, he stepped out of the car completely, waving his hand to me. My conflicted thoughts had shaken me downright. I was on the backseat while Mr. Jeeva was driving the vehicle. Just after 5 minutes, he parked the car and asked me to come to the pillion seat. "It feels like I am your driver. Would you mind joining me on the front seat? It would be effortless to interact with you." I, without uttering a word, unlocked the back door and slipped on the front seat. I rested my head on the right shoulder and peeped out of the window.

Mr. Jeeva asked, "How are you feeling now? What had happened that you had to de-board the bus?"

I turned my head towards him, suspiciously asking, "How do you know, I am not well? Who told you that we de-boarded the bus and were waiting at Noida Sec-51 bus stop?"

Mr. Jeeva started fumbling, "Ah, uh. Actually, Arijit was travelling on the same bus. He informed me."

"What? How come? He didn't even come to talk on me and wasn't he on vacation?" I asked angrily.

"Well... he was working on some other issue in the other building. I called off his holidays since you couldn't manage two sites. He must not have noticed you earlier, so he didn't speak to you, maybe. Your home is right here. Shall I help you to your room?" proposed Jeeva sir.

I denied rudely saying, "Thank you so much, sir. But I can walk through". I banged the door on his face.

Some vibrant energy was inherent inside, after having that suspicious conversation with Mr. Jeeva. I just unlocked my room and jumped onto my bed, throwing away the bag. A deep slumber invaded me pretty soon. Late evening, at 8:00 pm, on the same day, mom called me. It was here 6th call, which I finally managed to pick. "Hey, mom. Sorry I was sleeping. I haven't been keeping well. Had to work the entire night yesterday," I explained.

She replied angrily, "You aren't taking care of yourself. I guess I should come to visit you once to fix your life."

"I am fine mom, just a matter of the day. I will get back on track in no time. You don't worry, mom. I am going to cook some dinner. What do you think I should cook?" I played around.

She replied, "Just cook anything you know for your survival. I know you are not a chef yet. Hehehe."

There was a knock on the door. "Hmm. Ma, somebody is on the door. Shall I call you later?" I asked. Mom chuckled and hung up. I tied up my long hair, as I walked towards the door, opening it up. "Somebody is outside to see you," conveyed the security. I replied, "Alright, ask the person to wait in the visitor's lounge. I am coming." I hurriedly dressed up in a t-shirt and jeans, replacing my pyjamas. I saw Shahid as I entered the visitor's lounge and hugged him tightly.

"Shhh. It's ok. It's all fine. How are you now? I was worried about you," he spoke caressing my head with his one arm and holding me with the other.

I broke down into tears while saying, "I feel something is not right. Seriously, I don't know you. But I feel this strong connection with you in just one day."

Shahid comforted me, made me sit on the chair and sat right beside me. He chuckled, "Relax, I ain't any terrorist. I am your neighbour. I have been staying here for a year now. I saw you when you shifted. TCL is our client. I work in BT Communications, as a trainer. It's not that I am following you, but I really care for you and seeing you alone, struggling on your own, makes me worry for you. Rest, if you wish me to stay away from you, I can do that too. Just tell me, and I shall walk away from your life," Shahid spoke to me with a cute little smile on his face. I held his hand and said, "Thank you for thinking so selflessly about me. Not in today's world, everyone does that, without interests. Here is my number. Take a note."

Shahid pulled out his phone, opened up the keypad and handed over the phone to me. I dialled my number and saved it. I also rang myself through the same cell phone, so that I can catch hold of his number as well. It seemed as if I was enthralled by his charm and charisma. The meeting lasted no longer than 5 minutes. Shahid insisted me to take rest while he handed over dinner to me saying, "I have prepared it on my own, especially for you, considering that you aren't well today. I won't ask what had happened on the bus unless you want to talk about it. Rest, stay assured, I am not gonna blabber around about our new friendship." I urged him to stay for longer, but he denied saying, "It's 9:00 PM already, and you should be going. Even I have to wrap up for my presentation." We said goodbye to each other. I was smiling with loads of butterflies in my tummy. I sat back on my chair and started eating the yummy Biryani. With every bite it felt that life's greatest happiness is the conviction that we are loved; we are loved for being ourselves, or rather, loved in spite of being ourselves. Today, I know that all we really need to survive is one person who truly loves us. The night passed in the affectionate blues. Waking up to the fresh morning. I had a plethora of questions, but I just wanted to forget it as a dream of a devil. Shahid waved 'hi' to me from his apartment, and I waved back in reply with a big smile. Another day at the office— the 'Friyay' feeling. It was the day just after Diwali.

Colleagues are back. I met Sakshi, Sudarshan sir, Rakhi, Jai, Mannu, Vallabh, almost everyone in the team. But, there was one person I didn't want to meet today. That was Mr. Jeeva. Something felt suspicious about him. I knew that the chain of events was not natural, but had no proof against them.

I was working on the system, when Arijit said, "Hi, How are you?"

I replied in a busy tone, watching my order, "Yeah, I am good. How about you?".He scoffed saying, "How is the other guy, you have been hanging around with?"I skedaddled the place replying, "That's none of your business."

He followed me to the coffee station saying, "Hey, calm down. Just a question. Take it easy. I know there is nothing between you two."

"Who gave you the right to judge the relationship we share.

We could be lovers, friends, neighbours, anything," I quivered.

"That's what I mentioned. I guess I should catch you some other time," saying thisArjit vacated the breakout.

I grinned fiercely on his walkout. Friday didn't exactly feel like a 'yay' day, but office days can only be exciting when pigs fly. Shahid was standing right outside my office. I hurriedly ran to him, panting.

I said, "How come you are here?"

He replied, "Just to pick you up."

"Yeah, that's fine, but how long?" I questioned.

He scoffed and answered, "I can wait for you till eternity."

We burst into laughter, and I replied, "In your dreams. You flirt."

We had reached halfway on his motorcycle when my phone rang. I ignored it once, but it rang again.

I asked Shahid to pull over, pulling out the phone from my jeans, I questioned, "Yes, sir, what is it? I was on my way back home." "Pooja, ask your cabbie to turn back the car and get back to the office immediately. The client servers have crashed, and there is chaos going around. I am reaching the office in 5 minutes," replied Jeeva sir. "Hmm... Shahid you leave, I will take a cab back to the office. Something is wrong with the server. I got to bite this cherry, else the project will be handed over to somebody else," I advised Shahid. Shahid didn't agree on my taking a cab to the office. He was abstinent about dropping me back to the office. I didn't argue much, and he dropped me back to the office in no time. I hurried back to 5th floor. Mr. Jeeva was sitting at the coffee station as if he was waiting for me. I went to him and said, "What's wrong, sir? Is the server room open?"

"Pooja, being your manager, it's my duty to make sure that you are safe," remarked Jeeva sir.

"I didn't understand, sir," I uttered in confusion.

"Grab a seat and have this coffee," he said.

I took the bag off my shoulders and sat on the chair offered by him.

He continued, "The server issue has been taken care off since you returned quite late. Arijit is looking into it. But I want to talk about your cab schedule. The transport department updated me that these days you are not plying on cabs. Your security is my responsibility. Company is cautious and strict about the security of their female employees."

I was aghast at his words.

"But sir, I can commute on my own at times. Where on earth is it written on my offer letter that I can't travel on my own? The company owes me security and not spy service," I bashed his affirmation.

"You are an asset to TCL and me. By no means, I want to defame your identity here. I hope you understand what I am saying," he replied smartly.

I was pretty scared at this assertion of his and nodded my head in the consent of plying by cabs only. It was quite strange to see such a voracious appetite of disgust.

He asked, "Now, how would you commute back? Cabs won't be available from TCL at this time. So, let me drop you safely home."

I couldn't counter him and nodded 'yes'. We securely fastened the seat belts of the car and started from the office. Mr. Jeeva behaved differently, much different than my expectations. I used to see him as an ideal person, but the way he had been behaving for the last two days was signalling something fishy. I didn't talk to him at all during the travel. My sore eyes were craving for Shahid. It was a tall order which I had to abide by travelling with him. He turned on the music a little high. It was a love song. I felt like I was sitting in a duck's position, and anything can go wrong with me. The alert temperament in me had risen a notch above. Jeeva sir started, "So, Pooja, you know, I have been a huge fan of yours since the time I first saw you in office. That accident is so embedded in my memories. I can open up the album whenever I feel when you are not around. Your fervid attitude of living life with such independence drives me crazy." I didn't reply and was fluttering my eyeballs left, right, up and down to avoid eye contact. "It just took me a day to fall in love with a person like you," he continued.

"I am sorry, sir. But I guess you are not well this time. Or maybe you are not sure, whom you are talking to," I replied like a scared cat.

"I know it's like a snowball's chance in hell to get you, but I would do anything to win you because I really love you," he spoke in a heavy voice.

I boldly answered, "You got a family; a wife, two kids. I mean you have been married for 16 long years. How could you say such things? And if not you, I am guilty that because of me such malicious feelings arose in you. Please, pull over. I shall book a cab for myself," I cried.

Jeeva speeded up the vehicle and ordered me to put back the seat belt. I sat in the silent agony of being trapped with someone. Mr. Jeeva pulled over the car some 10 minutes behind my residence, in a quiet and sordid place. With tears in his eyes, he knelt, struggling around the space near the driving seat and begged me to accept his love. He said, "I know you are in no relationship. I know you are a virgin. I just want you to be mine forever. I am aware of the fact that I am married. But God only knows how much I love you. I love my family too, but since the time I have known you, my heart can't stop beating in your name."

I held his hands, which were trying to touch my feet, and replied, "It's ok. It's fine. I understand your urge to be with me. But I barely get time for a love affair. I have a lot to do, achieve in my life. Perhaps, getting trapped in a love line will distract me from my goals and motives."

"I understand. I shall not disturb you but all I want today a promise from you that you would spend just 5 minutes of yours every day with me. I believe 5 minutes won't be an act of Congress," he said

I pondered for a minute and replied in a warning, "Ok, but just 5 minutes."

He rejoiced in happiness. I had never envisioned Jeeva sir like this. Totally a different person I knew. Grasping my hand firmly in his, Jeeva spoke, "Today onwards, call me by any name and not 'sir'. Besides, if you don't mind, may I kiss you?"

I didn't know what to answer, and before I could say something, he brought his lips closer to mine, kissing them softly. He then removed my long hair from the right side of my shoulder, slipped down my t-shirt and kissed on my pointed shoulder. There was a current running down my body. Something like this had not happened to me before. I knew this was not right, but I had no ways to stop this. I immediately dressed my shoulder up and asked him to drop me home. He was the happiest man of the decade for he thought that he had convinced me for his love. I was disturbed at the very thought of falling in love with a man who is some 7-10 years older than me and to add to it, he is married. I reached my room and kept on turning, perplexed on my decisions.

CHAPTER 9
OLD WAS NOT GOLD

Against the grain, I had thought of Jeeva's new name. The next day was an off, and Jeeva rolled his wheels to my residence early morning at 8:30 AM. It was an off, and I had planned a lazy day. I snoozed up the alarm in every 5 minutes, resolute on getting up not before 8:30 AM. I wish I could have snoozed up my phone as well, which was ringing since 8:00 am. I finally opened my one eye, making sure that the other doesn't open up, answered my phone.

"Hey, sweety. I am right outside. Open up the window and say 'hi' to me", spoke J, alias Jeeva.

I swallowed my saliva like ants in my pants and replied, "Hi, J. I am still buried in my bed. I see you are outside. Allow me some time. I shall get back to you in some 15 minutes." Saying this I carelessly slept again, until the cellphone rang once more.

I answered it by saying, "I am getting ready."

J replied, "It's 10:30 now."

I woke up and changed my tone and said, "I will certainly be outside in 10 minutes." I collected my bucket, sprinkled water on me in 2 minutes, ran back to my room, dressed up in a midi. I locked my room hurriedly and slipping around the hurdles, presented myself to J. "I apologise for being so late," I spoke slowly.

I replied sarcastically, "It's ok. Perhaps, I should get used to it. Even my wife doesn't make me wait for so long."

"But what brings you here on an off so early?" I enquired.

He gave me a bouquet first, which he had hidden right behind him. Then, he answered, "I am here to take you out for a ride."

"Oh, thank you so much for the flowers, but ride, I mean I am not sure. It's not good to walk out publicly, as we work in an organization."

"Never mind, sweetheart, I can take care of it." He opened the car door for me, treating me like his lady. I smiled and stepped inside the car. He took his seat as well, and we started.

"I really liked my new name, J, sounds very modern. Thank you for considering my plea," he said.

"I am glad you liked it but where are we heading to?" I curiously inquired.

"We are going to the most elite restaurant in the city for lunch," he replied happily.

"Oh, it sounds good but I will have to be back by 2:30 PM. My mother is visiting me," I informed.

He responded disappointedly, "Oh, your mother. I see. No worries, I shall drop you on time."

I thanked him with gestures. We had a good lunch in those handful of 2 hours, and he dropped me back by 2:00 PM.

Meanwhile, I met Shahid on the way back to the room. He asked me, "Are you ok? How come you are on your own today?"

"Uh... Yeah, today, mom is arriving, was preparing for it. How about you?" I replied.

Shahid spoke, "Yeah, I am finally moving to Singapore for an exciting opportunity from my company."

"Really! Wow, so happy for you. New city, new life, new aspirations," I encouraged Shahid.

"But I shall miss you. Don't worry, will keep on visiting you over time. Till then, you hold on tight here," reassured Shahid.

I agreed in consent, taking each others' leave. 'Sigh, Shahid would leave. He is, indeed an ideal friend. More than I would have thought for Sachin Sachin is past now, maybe I shouldn't induce more pain, thinking about him,' I advised me. The clock is pacing up. Mom has arrived at the airport. She must be here in no time. I should hurry up. I fastened up and re-arranged the things in the room. Just in time, mom knocked on the door, and I hugged her with tears in my eyes. "I missed you, mom. Where had you been for so long?" I questioned in my childish tone. She kissed my forehead, held my waist and landed me onto the chair, wiping away my tears. She said, "I am here with you now. I have divorced your father. I got a job here and I am taking you to your new house." I was amazed. "Really, mom!" I asked unbelievingly. "You are the best mom on this earth," I applauded. My world changed in just 5 minutes. With Shahid leaving, I had perceived loneliness, which quickly shattered with mom entering into my life again. "Let me help you pack up. Our cab is waiting outside," ordered mother. The entire shift just took us an hour. I had the least and essential elements only for survival, which made our life terribly easy while packing. I was behaving like a babe in arms. The cab was loaded with the luggage and a new family towards a new beginning. Within 45 minutes, we arrived at the new flat situated in the prime location of the city. It took us two days entirely to relocate to the new place and my vacations were consumed. My happiness knew no bounds. The two days off were over, and it was time to get back to the salt mines. I returned to the office. The happy hours with mom made me forget that I even carried a cell phone. There were 777 missed calls from J. There were also calls from my old residence. I entered the office and found J extremely angry. He was precisely not in a mood to talk to me. The moment I carried my laptop to him for a brief discussion, he boiled up, and shouted, "Don't you see I am in another meeting." I retired back to my seat, thinking about how to explain that I got swamped and had to shift in a hurry. I sat quietly with tears rolling down my cheeks. I knew we are like chalk and cheese, non-compliant to each other's behaviour. Still, there was something which compelled me to keep trying to talk to him. My patience was rewarding. He returned to me, showing the number of calls he made, to which I politely replied, "I told you mom had come. I just got no time to inform you that she is back from Varanasi and she had purchased a new house in Noida. She helped me pack, and we have permanently settled in Sec-15 now. Just mom and I." He answered, "It was effortless for you Pooja, to spare a minute, call me and say, J, I am moving from this place to Sector-15 Noida. I would have done it if I had been at your place. It would have hardly taken some 5 minutes." I comforted him, caressing his foot with mine, and said, "I am sorry. I will bear in mind. Please, stop being so ignorant of me." His touches of sarcasm were quite decipherable throughout the day in almost everything he said to me. I was clear in mind that he would beat me to the draw until I abide by his words. Gradually, with each passing day, our closeness increased with some vague conditions. Love was a routine phone call to update the other about the daily chores, inclusive of locations and sleep timings. Every day, we would converse late at night, tell each other almost everything about the day, even when we spent nearly 40% of the day together. J would drop me home after office, hugging me and kissing my lips. Things were rolling fresh until Shahid returned to India for a small family break. The very first day, he expressed his wish to meet me, making a call. I was in the office like every other day. Shahid was supposed to arrive by 3:00 PM. I thought about taking a half-day. Hence, I visited J's cabin, to narrate the reason for a half-day leave. J angrily replied, "I agree Shahid is a perfect friend of yours, but I am not convinced with your half-day leave reason. Stay back, complete your backlog." I returned to my seat, burning in anger. Shahid had made four calls, but I didn't pick up in the guilt of not being able to make up to him. The clock struck 4:45 pm. I was sitting in the office, watching my phone, while J was watching me. I banged the system in anger, packed my bag and left the office. J ran behind me. I maintained a quicker pace this time to escape his clutches, but all my efforts were in vain. By that time, almost the entire office knew that something was budding up between J and me, which I didn't like. I was behind the eight, which was another reason for me to stop at J's first call from behind. "Pooja, Pooja, please, stop." I halted, panting heavily. J crossed me and questioned, "Why are you in a hurry? Your office leaving time is 5:30 PM. How dare you leave without bidding goodbye?" Arijit was watching it close with all ears and eyes wide open. I replied screamingly, "My friend has called me 5 times. I should be going. He isn't here for months, just for three days. I have to meet him."

I replied, "Either I will drop you, or you stop seeing me from today. I will take an exit from your life."

I was in between a rock and a hard place. I replied, "Why do you do this to me? I love you, but that doesn't mean you will dominate everywhere."

He softly said, "It's your call now. Either wait here till I bring my car or leave me forever."

I agreed with dismay and sat back near the reception. The moment he left, Arijit came close to me asking, "Is everything ok with you?" I fumbled and said, "Yeah, it's all ok." He nodded his head. The story which started as a 5-minutes meeting has now turned out to be a havoc of 5 lifetimes. I was struggling between commitment and freedom. If I chose freedom, I would have to betray commitment, and if I chose commitment, freedom would never get back to me.

J rang me the sooner, he reached the floor. I picked up his call, to which he spoke, "Are you ok, alone there? Is anyone bothering you? Tell me. I shall kill that guy. Somebody informed me that Arijit came closer to you. Did he say anything to you? Tell me. I am coming in 15 minutes. Don't worry, Pooja. I am coming."

I softly spoke, "I am fine."

The clock struck 5:30, and J drove his car through the exit, while we were engaged in a call. I had received 2 calls from Shahid and one call from mom, but I wasn't allowed to overshadow his call with anyone. I covered myself up and walked straight to his car. I opened the door and sat beside him. He turned on the music loud. I didn't utter a word.

He asked, "What makes you so quiet? I believe nothing is more important than me to you because we are in a relationship. Isn't it?"

I didn't reply. He pulled over the car and denied to drive unless I talk it out with him. I said, "My friend was waiting for me. I am pissed because of that. He has been calling me because he was already at my house and now thanks to you, Shahid has left."

J smiled and replied, "So what's the big deal. Let's go and meet him at his house. You can introduce me to your friend, Shahid." I finally agreed not to meet Shahid. J denied me offs, and Shahid was returning on an early morning flight on Saturday. This time, every day at the office turned more hectic. I was biting off more than I could chew. Appraisals were announced on Friday evening. People were in carousing mood. Almost everyone, including Sudarshan, got 25% increment, while I was promoted to the position of assistant manager with a 27% increment. Sakshi, Mannu, Sudarshan sir, everyone congratulated me and demanded a party.

Rakhi, Vallabh, Jai and Arijit were not happy with my upgraded position. There were rumours in the office that I have compromised my values for this promotion. People had been talking about my affair with J, thanks to Arijit and also J. I broke down after hearing all the commotion about my defamation. Never had I imagined that life would be so unfair. J was worried too, but somewhere because of his pathetic and careless behaviour. People undermined my true potential. Seeing me all worried, J, consoled me saying, "Pack your stuff up, we are leaving for Chandigarh today."

I stared at him. "I put up with my mother. What on earth, shall I say in perfect pretext?" I spoke grinning.

He winked and replied, "I shall cover you up". I gave a lost look. J opened up his laptop and drafted an email, which read:

"Hi,

The R&D team is aligned for a collateral meeting with Havel Pvt. Ltd. in Chandigarh, for which attendance is mandatory for all the team members. This meeting shall start w.e.f Saturday morning and would end on Monday morning.

Please, make all the prior preparations. The flight tickets can be obtained from the travel desk. Please, assemble early morning at 6:00 am in the office premises.

Regards,
Jeeva Shinghal,
Manager- R&D"

He forwarded the mail to me and asked me to show it to my mother. I was amazed at his insinuating wit. The plan worked, and mom agreed for my departure to Chandigarh. This was the first time I was travelling with someone, whom I had known only for a few months. The most intriguing thing was, I agreed to go out with him, which I shouldn't have. But this love is a disease, you are sick, and you don't feel it. I was in love with him, but somewhere, I felt the blockage, I never wanted to suffer. The plane was ready to fly. The only modification was that it had no wings but four wheels. I was in a party mood. So was he! The journey started with some snacks and coke.

Munching was on with music served loud. J was driving, and I was dancing. Phones were on 'do-not-disturb' mode. Bash was high on "Zing-Zing-Zingat" with the best car choreography. Fleeting hands from left to right and then again from right to left, we could have been selected easily in Indian Idol for being the best dancing 'Jodi'(Couple). But then, the phone rang, it was Arijit. I paused the music and received the call. "Hey, Arijit! How are you?" I started.

"Hey, Pooja. What's up? Let's catch up today evening! I was thinking, it has been 11 months since you joined the team, and we should really catch up sometimes outside."

I knew on hearing this, J would burst up. I replied, "I can hear you by the margin of my nose. I am out with mom today. I will connect with you later. Bye."

I hung up. I turned up the music and starting shaking when J turned down the volume and interrupted, "Who was he?"

I replied, "It was Arijit."

"Why did he call?" questioned J.

"He just wanted to discuss some office stuff. So, he called. I told him that we can deal with it on Monday," I smiled while saying this. J pulled over the car and stepped out of the vehicle, stood with folded hands. I wondered why he was behaving like that. I stepped out of the wheels, unfastening my seat belt. "What's wrong with you?" I asked irritatingly. He wasn't in the mood to utter a word. I held J's hand firmly, forcing him to turn his face towards me. "Look at me and talk to me," I shouted. On the highway, under the dark sky, with the gushing wind and vehicle speeding with air, I wanted him to answer. After a long pause and repeated blood and thunder, J spoke, "You are lying to me. I know he asked you out."I replied, "Even if he had, I denied. Isn't it? Then, why are you blowing your top? I didn't tell you the truth because I knew you would overreact."

J rushed back into the car and grab hold of my phone. He asked me for the password. I said, "Why the hell do you need the password. Am I supposed to summon to you this way?" He blew the stack and screamed for the password. I unwillingly shared it with him. The moment he got the password, he unlocked the phone, and read my text messages, WhatsApp, call logs, gallery and almost everything. After 5 minutes of scrolling, he ensured that I had no past conversations with Arijit. He smiled and returned my phone. Out of the blue, J's phone rang. It was his wife calling. He steered his fingers on my lips, asking me to stay silent until the call gets over.

The other side of the phone spoke, "Hey honey, where are you?"

J replied, "I am still stuck in some emergncy. I maybe busy today and tomorrow with the same. That's why I am not returning home tonight. Will return on Monday morning. By the way, how's your health? Where are my stars, Jahaan and Ashna?"

The other side of the phone again replied, "Alright then, we shall party tonight, since it's Friday. I am also taking my regular medicines. Both Jahaan and Ashna are doing fine. Both of them are missing you a lot."

Jahaan and Ashna shout from behind, "We miss you, Papa. Come soon. We know you are very busy. Please, take good care of yourself, Papa."

J replied with a kiss, "Me too, my prince and princess."

J then disconnected the phone. He said, "I am sorry for this behaviour, but I hate liars. I have learnt not to lie, and I am coaching my daughter and son, not to lie, too, to anyone ever. Hope you bear this in mind." I nodded in consent, but I knew I have borrowed trouble. We got back into the vehicle, and the journey started once again. Throughout the way on the expressway, he held my hand with one hand and the steering with the other, expressing the importance of my touch for him. I was focused more on my cell phone, praying to God to stop landing calls on my cell. Although I was sure, he won't leave me midway, but somewhere the fear of getting tormented by his weird behaviour was scaring me off the bump in the road. I smiled at nearly everything he said. Hunger and nature calls impeded our journey, but we sort of enjoyed the street food and the jungle explorations. We reached Chandigarh finally at 6:30 PM. We secured our room in the hotel and hit the sack. J claimed me to be his wife and had booked a deluxe bedroom. Our imprints were already taken at the reception. The breakfast for both days was complimentary.

Tired till toe, I insisted on sleeping first. So, we hurriedly finished our dinner at a nearby restaurant. The phone call by Arijit was a hot potato. Every time my cell phone rang, I prayed it to be my mother only. This time, on the dinner table, it rang again. I watched J hesitantly. He handed over the phone to me, saying, "It's your mom's. Why don't you pick and tell her everything is fine." The cost of the entire travel was borne by J. I wasn't competent enough to contribute to the gambol. J was earning a massive salary, nearly 45 lakhs, sufficient to take care of such petty trips.

The other ping-pongs, email and app notifications were regularly addressed by J. My phone was no longer my property. He would make sure to carry it in his pocket, pretending to be a manager at service. All my neighbourhood friends, some flirts and at times, Shahid, kept on texting on and off. This was really annoying to see him peep at my phone every time it buzzed. The dinner was tasty, but the dining experience wasn't so good, especially with regular phone inspections. We returned to the room. I took the lead in making the necessary arrangements before sleep. It included brushing my teeth, changing the dress, putting on my night suit and finding a space to sleep.

I cast the first stone in the washroom, brushed my teeth, dressed up in my pyjamas and sat right next to J. J was busy checking my text messages. I knocked. He didn't reply. I hit again, "I will sleep on the bed. You catch the sofa." He ignored, busy checking through the travel photos. I said, "Please, get off. I wish to sleep." He locked the phone in a chuffed fashion and replied, "I am not sleeping on the sofa. We are here to sleep together." I revolted, "This is not right. I agree that I love you, but I just can't get physical with you." I got off from the bed and sneaked in the balcony, looking at the moon. He followed me, slamming the slider of the gallery.

CHAPTER 10
TRAPPED VIRGINITY

He hugged me from behind, kissing my right ear. I shivered in excitement and pushed him off me. J tried to hold me again, this time with a firmer grip, kissing my neck from behind. Slowly reverberating in my ear, "I love you. I just can't hold myself when I am looking at you. Please, say you are just mine."

His cock was growing big and was touching my thighs. I could feel some hot fluid oozing out. He grabbed my breasts above my clothes and pulled me inside the room. I could feel him growing hard and big with every kiss he landed on my body. He threw me on the bed and started kissing my thighs, moving to the v-point gradually. I tried to move, but it felt like he had tied me up with some invisible thread.

The tsunami was sure to drown me today. J's tongue was turning aggressive, traversing uphill. His fingers were rolling over my T-shirt while his tongue was sweeping me off my feet. A round-robin vogue was played by his tongue, while his teeth would pinch out the scream off me. His fingers were now marking down their territories on my breast, steadily pinching my left nipple. I shouted with pleasure, which he contemplated as pain. He left the sordid tit and grabbed my left corner, turning me towards him. He asked softly, "I am sorry. Did I hurt you? Are you ok? I reckon I must have pinched you hard." I replied with a nod that I was fine. J hugged me tight and asked me to sleep. But his dick was tight seeking for a warm tunnel of heaven. I could feel it as it was touching my v-point. I didn't move and laid feeling insecure, wondering what if he rapes me? I pretended to sleep. J wasn't sleeping either. He wanted me to fall asleep soon so that he can start playing around for orgasm. J's excitement was at the top-notch. To clean the air, he stepped out of bed and started walking inside the room with small steps. Staring at me every 5 minutes. He was cooling down his heels. I fell asleep in some 15 minutes, and there were crickets around. He secretly rolled over the bed without making any screeches and approached very close to me. He was watching me, tranquillizing his doubts about me; still awake. Once he ensured that I was dead asleep, J started undressing me. J unbuttoned the shirt first successfully. He then tried to loosen my bra but failed. He re-attempted, making sure that I don't wake up. But, all his efforts were in vain. He scoffed in disappointment and stepped out of bed again. He again roamed for a minute but returned with the same enthusiasm of undressing me. He tried to cut it open but in some different way. Luck favoured me again, defeating his ugly intentions. I was dead asleep, unaware of the things happening with me. He decided to change horses in the midstream and targeted my v-point. He stepped out of bed again, this time holding himself against my feet. He started pulling off my pyjamas from my feet at a controlled pace. After a second, the pyjamas started slipping down my waist, then, down my thighs, nearly exposing my pantyhose. J was chasing rainbows because he didn't know that he has meddled with Pooja. I felt like I was robbed of my clothes. I woke up in distress, and said, "What the hell are you doing?" J stepped back and turned towards the gallery door. I slept again. He realised sex with me is like a cold day in July. But he was in the seventh heaven, appreciating his reach to my private parts at least. That night, J was restless and extremely excited. Somewhere deep down, he realized that I was hard to get. Early morning at 5:00 AM, mother's call woke us up. I picked the call saying, "Good morning, mom. I just woke up. Rushing to an office meeting. I shall call you back once free. The other phone, which was J's, rang, too, just after 5 minutes. It was Satakshi calling, J's wife. She chose to video call, which J rejected screaming, " I am not in the mood to talk right now. Let me sleep more. Will call you once I am up." Both of us were lying motionless in an obtuse angle. J finally took the call and said, "Let's get up.

We need to roam around a lot. First, we will have breakfast, then we will visit the Rock Garden and finally, to the lake." I just replied with a 'hmm'. We were silent again for 5 minutes. My phone rang again. This time it was Shahid on the call. I walked into the washroom to pick up the call, without disturbing J. He was still in a deep slumber. Shahid asked about my well-being and informed me about his next visit to India. I exchanged my new achievement with him, and we both decided to definitely meet and celebrate. I brushed my teeth, took a shower and finally found J on the washroom door. "What are you doing here?" I asked in surprise. He replied, "I wanted to get inside too." I took a breath of sigh for I knew J didn't realise that Shahid called. Aware of J's dead eye, I had anticipated the consequences of him knowing that Shahid called. I pushed him into the shower and forced him to dress up. The clock struck 10:20 am. "Breakfast is gonna get over by 10:30 am. Can we please, hurry up?" I shouted in concern. In no time, J brushed his teeth, and we were out of the room on our way to the buffet in just 5 minutes. We made it dot on time. Our breakfast was saved. We hurriedly collected the food of our choices in different plates and comforted ourselves over a sofa. I was dressed up in nine, which of course called for fellow dwellers' attention. A guy in a yellow T-shirt was staring me, driving me up the ball. I complained, "That gentleman in yellow is staring me again and again." J freckled and replied, "It's you who is staring him. Stop pretending as if you are the prettiest." J blocked my view by changing his seating position. I turned my head down and started eating. We didn't talk until we completed the food. We returned to the room. I grabbed a corner of the bed and started checking my office emails. J stood in front of me, saying, "I am sorry for cutting you off during breakfast. I just hate when you check guys around. You are just mine, and your attention should always be on me." I frowned and didn't reply. He abducted my phone, slipped it in his pocket and hugged me, asking for forgiveness. I replied, "Please, return my phone. I will make sure that I don't share things with you that you don't like." He said, looking straight into my eyes, "From your hair strand to the nail of your toe, every inch of your body belongs to me. Do you understand?" The inveterate situation was arbitrated by a phone call from Satakshi. J answered the call, "Hey, sweetheart. Sorry I was asleep when you called. Yeah, everything is fine. I am missing you too. I love you too. Please, take the kids out for some Saturday fun. Use my card for any expenses. Bye. Take care." J turned back to me, "Sorry! So, where were we? Let's get going, we have to travel a lot." I agreed in search of some change. We stepped in the car and roamed around the city. Our first halt was the Rock Garden, which was pretty big to cover in a day. We clicked pictures around the artificial forts and seas. Almost everything you could imagine of was carved out in waste material. I felt that was a mandatory place to visit in Chandigarh. Almost more than half of the day was consumed. We were left with some odd 4 hours before the dark would prevail. We grabbed some street bite after rock garden and headed towards the lake. J held my hand, walking with me like we were a couple. I wondered what people would think about us. About me? That I didn't find any suitable bachelor of my age. Such thoughts were quite disturbing in the beginning. But love knows no age barrier. His affection beckoned me. Regular calls from mother and Satakshi were a habit now.

We would find some peaceful place and talk to them as if we were actually working at the office. Another day spent successfully and we made the best fools of our families. A collected a plethora of pictures with loads of memories. We returned to the hotel at 9:30 PM. Both of us were hungry, and hence, we headed straight to the restaurant. J gave me an option of buffet or Al-Carta. I chose the buffet. We attacked the buffet and ate almost everything arranged at our service. The sweets were the delight of the night. We grabbed a bagful of sweets and retired back to the room with bloated stomachs. The night drove J wild again, but he was in no state to move left or right. Erstwhile, he slept, snoring high, the moment his head rested on the bed. I was at peace and happy that I finally fled the night attacks. I pulled over the blanket, stuck beneath his feet and spread it over along his body. I followed my regular chore, brushed my teeth, changed the dress and grabbed the right corner of the bed. Finally, today, I can also sleep carelessly. I played around some app notifications in calmness and slept once done. I wasn't used to snores but managed somehow. I had set the alarm for early morning, at 5:00 AM, so that our early departure could help us reach Delhi city by 11:00 AM max.

We woke up to the shrieking voice of the alarm. We hurriedly used the washroom, packed up and left for our destination. J was holding my hand throughout the route, caressing it softly, telling me the importance of the sensation of touch. It was challenging to understand the science of touch for me. But, I was slowly getting used to it. He added moons to the journey by reciting some very famous dialogues from the movie like— "I know I love you since centuries, it's just that it took years to find you. You are the best thing in my best days." I was astonished by his sense of romance and commented, "You must have been the filmiest lover of your time." He smiled with a complete teeth show off and replied, "I am lucky to have both you and Satakshi in my life." Thankfully, nothing weird happened on the way back home, maybe because my phone didn't ring or I didn't say anything which he didn't like.

We returned to the city safely and headed directly to the office. I stepped out of the vehicle a Kilometer ahead so that nobody would doubt that I was with him, while he drove his car to the parking lot. The office started on a hectic note as there were backlogs of the last week. Back to back meetings were tiring and hence, I took the cab sharp at 5:00 pm for home. J was in a meeting. I called him, but he couldn't pick since he was presenting the financial deck to the management. I left the office and was about to board the cab when Arijit called me from behind, "Hey, Pooja. Hey, Pooja." I turned back and saw Arijit. His gestures made me understand that he wants to drop me home. I was worried on hopping in his car, for I knew that J would again get furious.

I gave it a second thought, and made gestures, denying him the ride. He started honking and shouting. "Uh… Alright, alright I am coming," I signalled him to stop. Cancelling the Uber cab, I hopped into Arijit's car. Arijit made immediate haste and sped up like light. I boggled at this attitude and asked him to slow down. Arijit didn't reply. I asked, "What's wrong with you?" Arijit was only focused on escaping the place. "What surprise is this? Are you planning to show me something," I asked again. Arijit hit my nose hard in response. "Are you insane?" I questioned madly while holding my bleeding nose. He gave me another blow on my head, followed by a repeated hit on my face. I was defending his hit with both my hands and elbows but all in vain. I had no idea how to fight this fire. To add on, his finger pointing statements made me fly off the handle. I could only hear him saying in repetition, "I love you, and you are sleeping around with that bastard, Jeeva. I loved you madly, and you got your hand on my Associate Manager's position also. I shall punish you for this." From pillar to post, he was driving madly. Jeeva and mom were calling me repeatedly, but I was all handicapped. I tried to pick my phone, slipping out of his sight, but time didn't favour me. He snatched away the phone and threatened to throw it out of the window if I didn't abide by what he said. My entire face was swollen, and my eyes were severely hurt. After a hustle of an hour, he kicked me out of his car near the office road. A crowd gathered around me and helped me to get to the nearest hospital. This was the most dreadful episode of my life. I was lying motionless and unconscious, unable to explain the incident. Mother was weeping, and Jeeva was on call, that's what I could see with the swollen eyes. It took me two days to recover completely. Every colleague of my team and some office mates from different groups visited the hospital to enquire about my well-being. Mother was helping me to get back on my feet while Jeeva would stay all night long in the hospital to guard me and ensure my security. Finally, I expressed my wish to narrate the incident to my mother and Jeeva. I explained to them how Arijit ambushed me in the car and blew fists on my face with a bag full of allegations. Mother stared Jeeva with suspicion. Jeeva escaped her sight, cutting a sorry look and pretending that he was utterly unaware of what had been going on. He returned to the office in search of Arijit but came to know that Arijit had left the city already. A police complaint was made against Arijit, and I returned home from the hospital. Mother strictly asked me to put down papers of TCL and stay back home. She had lost confidence in Jeeva and office management. She didn't want to lose me to scavengers like Arijit as I was her only prized possession. For the time being, Jeeva stopped visiting me at home. He even stopped calling me and d ropping any messages. Somewhere, my mother understood that Jeeva might have had something to do with what happened with me. I was free to do anything but I was missing Jeeva in certain aspects, I am not sure what. We never gelled up well or geared up in sync, but this love was different than what I usually find people falling into.

CHAPTER 11
THE BDSM OF LIFE

I took a week off from office to remove the effects of misprisions of a felony, which included the offence of failing to report forceful conduct. Sitting by my window, I felt like I went cold turkey. I was addicted to J's dominating love. Life seemed to be a role-play of a perfect BDSM, where I was playing a submissive slave. The romance was enthralling with pains of satirical inspections. The roots of the investigation were embedded in extreme ends of my body, as J had mentioned earlier. I had the liberty to shout, but only after a spank by J. He hasn't compromised any authoritative position in this role-play affair. He was writing the Bible rule book of love between a middle-aged man and a young, virgin girl. The stereotype of girls, happy to share squalid and dingy flats was a thing of the past. Spending almost 6 months with J, the idea that love is not freeing but enslaving me was the increasing germane. Wounds were healing but not on heart.

On the Contrary, J had to ensure that his office performance doesn't drop even by a point. Being a manager, he had a lot of teams to look after, but in every group, his eyes would hunt for me. His eyes on the screen and the office entrance door, thinking that I would arrive any day. At times, to quench his love polydipsia, J would park his car outside my apartment, standing there for hours to get a glimpse of me. In a regular stride for fresh air, I often visited the balcony. I could easily spot his vehicle from the balcony and inside it, J, getting out of his limb, to catch a 5-minute glimpse of mine. Love was turning into a possessive clandestine affair every 5 minutes. He made it a routine to park outside my apartment to catch a glimpse of me on and off.

J was ignorant of his family and children. Every day, he would return home drunk and distracted as if he is heart-broken, going in a pear shape. He was grasping stones now, by asking my colleagues to call me and hand the phone to J after a small conversation. In last one week,

I have received calls from almost everyone, Mannu, Sakshi, Jai, Rakhi and even Sudarshan sir. After the first introduction, they would hand over the phone to J. J would sob on calls, beg me to return to the office. "I cannot live without you", went viral in my ears with every request. But, my numb senses won't reply. I was in melancholy of being addressed as his mistress.

People in the office already knew of his inclination towards me, making me insecure about my self-respect in the office. The rough and animalistic behaviour of Arijit resounds the opinion of the office colleagues about my lose character. Does falling in love with J makes me incompetent? Don't I deserve my Associate Manager position? These questions were haunting me like a serial killer. I finally decided to extend my leaves, dropping an email addressed to J. The sooner the mail landed in his inbox, J reverted with the message, "Don't do this to me, honey. I am going Bananas without you. I will spoil everything if you don't get back as early as possible. Satakshi has already started doubting me. I can't hold it anymore. Please, get back to me. Missing you. Your's, J." A new hope arose for J, sending messages on email, which would stay untracked atleast by my mother. I decided not to reply to the emails he kept on dropping in my mailbox over the days. From the office mailbox to the personal mailbox, all were spammed up by his 'missing you' emails.

I wanted to reply, but I knew this won't be good for us. J was getting high on his nerves, unable to bear my cold shoulder towards him. He decided to drink to death, one excellent evening after the office. "Today, unlimited alcohol would be my poison," he committed to himself. He grabbed a chair close to the bar counter and drank heavily. He couldn't control his emotions and started ringing me back to back like a hail mary. I ignored his calls and turned the cell ringer to silent. Calls followed by appeals left his hope hanging by a thread, but I didn't pick his call. J was now 10 bottles down, having his head in clouds. He could barely walk or speak. He helped himself to the car and slept right after securing his seatbelt. His situation was critical, and he needed immediate medical attention. But none came to his rescue.

J lied unconscious in the car for almost 2 hours. Satakshi grew worried and started calling mutual contacts. None of them knew where J was. Perturbed with no news of J till 2:00 am, Satakshi rang her in-laws and called for help. J's family lived around the corner. With the report, the family summoned at his house, waiting for him fervently. J gained consciousness at 2:40 AM, mustering the courage to drive back home. Somehow, he managed to reach home and kept on falling at a lot of places from the parking lot to his apartment. He had a nose for finding directions, which landed him straight on his door where he lied flat. The doors were open with worried and weeping faces, peeping from inside. Satakshi ran to him, "Jeeva, What's wrong? Are you ok? Are you drunk?" she sobbed and asked. Jeeva hauled over the coals saying, "Get off me. I am fine." J's father helped him on his feet and carried him to the bed. With every boastful word of J, the entire room stunk like a dead cat. J was high on alcohol, everyone had perceived by now. Satakshi loosened his shoes, removed his socks and changed his dress. Every time Satakshi touched him, J replied, "Pooja, why did you leave me? I can't live without you, Pooja. Please, come to me, Pooja". Hearing this, tears rolled down Satakshi's cheeks, but she didn't tell this to J's parents. Kids were sleeping in the other room, unaware of the happenings around. Satakshi closed J's room to ace up her sleeves. She talked to J's parents, comforting them that everything was ok, and he has returned from an office party. By fair means or foul, she persuaded them to believe that everything is fine. J's parents returned the same night. I was also restless the entire night, praying for J's well being, but didn't want to convey this to him to weaken him more. Love is a toxic substance which secretes potions of telepathy, connecting two lovers by any means. I was aware that J has done something wrong to himself. Late morning, J woke up. By that time, Satakshi had already sent the kids to school. She didn't wake J up. J stretched a bit and shouted, "Satakshi, Where is my Coffee? It's 9:40 already. Why didn't you wake me up for the office?" Satakshi ignored his screeches and continued her work in the kitchen. "Why isn't she answering me. I can hear the turbulent noises from the kitchen," J whispered to himself. He got off the bed and pulled open the door, approaching close to Satakshi. "Hey, are you deaf? I am screaming for the last 5 minutes?" J addressed Satakshi. Satakshi didn't reply, acting deaf.

J held her sleeves and shook her hard saying, "Are you crazy?" Satakshi jolted high, "Yes, I am crazy because I am into helicopter parenting and you are flying as high as a kite. By the way, you didn't tell me anything about Pooja." "What...What... Poo...Pooja?" fumbled and stumbled Jeeva in his speech. "I know what your office parties and meetings are all about," answered Satakshi, throwing a cup. Jeeva shouted, "Mind your language. There is nothing between Pooja and I. It just happened in the last meeting that Pooja misbehaved with me and I was missing you that time. I was calling out your name but must have mingled both the names in high disposition." He held on to Satakshi's shoulders with both the hands and said in her ears, "You are everything to me, and nothing on this earth can take your place. Get these jerks off your brains, stop hitting the roofs." Satakashi, calmed down after hearing this, agreeing to whatever J spoke for the time being. But, she wanted to confirm her benefit of the doubt given by Jeeva. That day, Jeeva took an off; however, he left no stone unturned in connecting with me via emails. He laid on the bed all day long, staring at my profile pictures on all the social media platforms; from Instagram to LinkedIn.

Satakshi, hovering around, ready to hit the sack after a long day tiring work at home, caught J staring at my photos. "Why are you watching Pooja's photo?" questioned Satakshi with the gestures of handing over the phone to her. J was in a Hobson's choice. He had to either accept that it is Pooja or hand the phone over to Satakshi. J played smart, saying, "Yes she is Pooja, I was checking if she commented on any of my pictures as she mentioned last night." Satakshi smiled in doubt without uttering a word. J clearly escaped the second time.

Meanwhile, later in the evening, my mother returned home with a long sad face. She was in a hot mess with some home truths. I carried a glass of water and politely asked, "Is everything ok, Ma?"

Mom drank some water and broke into tears again. I grasped her firmly, consoling her sobs. "Just tell me, Ma, everything will be alright. I am here for you," I added. "I quit my job today," said mom weeping on a higher pitch. I consoled her again, saying, "You will find another one. Calm down, Ma. It's nothing big. But, why did you quit your job," I questioned mother. She wiped her tears off her saree's loose end and said, "The director asked for physical favours in return of hike." I skipped a breath, thinking, "Is my mom that strong to put her job on stake just for her self-respect."Tears rolled down my cheeks, and I started crying. Mother immediately stopped weeping and encouraged me, saying, "Don't worry, daughter. I will find another job. This was something which I wasn't expecting at this point of age, which compelled me to burn out the aggression inside in tears. Fear not, we will handle this situation. You are my strongest daughter, my asset," mother said and hugged me tightly. After hearing mom, I was in a fog, thinking if I should have taken the same call. J is already married to someone, in high commitments with his children. I have made a blunder. How could I fall in love with someone who is cheating on his family? I have now started living in guilt of depriving people of their rights. This relationship between J and I was a complete wash. I also knew it takes two to tango, so I decided to withdraw from support from this relationship. I felt as I was in the toilet all day. I was on leaves without pay now. It was almost 21 days that I had been home. Mom tried her luck at most of the places but was denied the offer because of the influential director who wasn't given the favours. He ensured that mom wouldn't find a job anywhere. Mother wanted to file a criminal case against him, but she was already dealing with her divorce case in the court, which would have made the situation adverse.

I had to jump the gun now, ensuring that we don't run out of all our savings. I finally decided to get back on work. Right after 23 days, I punched my card in the office. Colleagues looked happy after my return and welcomed me for a healthy recovery. J was waiting for me in his cabin with his arms wide open. But, I didn't see him on my arrival, neither did I call him. J couldn't underpin this insult. He banged on my desk with an issue saying, "First you were on uninformed leave for 25 days, and second, you haven't addressed any problems in the last 2 hours. Where the fuck is your mind? If you think, you can't handle it, tell me. I will offer this position to someone responsible". The entire office started looking at my desk.

I started weeping. Never had this happened in the whole working career that I had been abused for my work? J realised that he over-reacted. He apologised to everyone sitting there and asked me to follow him to the meeting room. I wiped my tears and followed J to the meeting room. J offered me a glass of water and apologised, "I am sorry for losing temper. I was dying to touch you, to hold you, to see you. Don't you know you are my lifeline? Why didn't you reply to my messages, my mails and my calls? Don't you love me anymore?" He fired a lot of questions, and for the first time, I didn't know what to reply. I maintained my calm, saying, "I am suffering too in a lot of ways. I was in problem, and I didn't want you to land in my questions. I love you, but our paths are different. Practically, we should stop dating and start focusing on our works." "What could have been more relevant to you than me? Why did you leave me? I was dying in your separation, and you were enjoying at home updating your Instagram and WhatsApp account pictures. What a shame you are? I know now, you need new people every day in your life. You think you are the prettiest lady. You would sleep with me in just Rs.200/." Everything he said appeared poison to my ears. I almost vomited, but I controlled my emotions just to ensure no scenes are made in the office again.

I started weeping again. J stumbled and said, "Don't cry, please, you are my princess, right? But you shouldn't have treated me like a piece of shit."

I replied, "I wish to resign. I have prepared a letter in drafts. Please, approve it for further proceedings."

"Did you get another offer? I knew you are such a liar and such a cheat. How much are they offering? When did you go for an interview? Oh, I see that's why you took 25 days off to prepare for another interview. Such a bitch, you are," he shouted.

I scoffed and replied, "I have no offer in hand. I just wish to resign."

J changed his tone, speaking, "I can't let you resign without any offer. However, if you have any suggestion, show me the offer letter and then leave. Just for the record, I know your mother has also lost her job."

"How do you know?" I asked, amazed.

"I am a lover, and I know everything in and out. One of your apartment residents works under me. I made him a friend and enquired about you. He updates me about you, all your movements with your in and out times of the apartment. So I advise, support your mom, stay back, and drop the idea of resignation. With this pace, in a year or two, you will be crowned the manager of the R&D department," he said.I was choked out of fresh thoughts. I felt so weak in front of the situation, and I returned to work. J had started pressing hard on me with work. Routine tasks were taking a toll. So, he indulged me in his night activities as well. Every day I would spend the entire day working in his cabin. Anybody willing to talk or discuss things with me was abashed by J badly. The team had almost entirely stopped talking to me, even Sudarshan, in fear of either losing their job or getting dragged by J. I was completely in J's custody. Late night, J would stay up with me on video calls in place of work. Mother was watching it all but kept mum. She was trying hard to hold on to some job, but all in vain. I started staying engaged all day from the moment I entered the office. J left no stone unturned in making sure that he remains my world forever. I wasn't allowed to attend lunch parties with my colleagues. Even if J would be in some meeting, he would ask me to wait for him. Every day, he would remind me of my atrocities to him in the past 25 days. I was craving for sleep. My routine revolved around him every day. I had almost made my mind to resign.

CHAPTER 12
LUST TRADES WITH GREED

But looking at mom and the daily expenses, my priority was to find a high paying job. I started applying for interviews at different companies. J knew I was doing this. He didn't want me to leave the company, most importantly, the team. The golden days of love would burst into pieces, so J started keeping me at bay from other interviews. He proposed, "If I get your mom a job, will your problem be solved? I know you have been working hard to get a high paying job, but with just 1.2 years of experience in the industry, you won't be able to make it. You have to at least establish an experience of a minimum of 2 years to get rid of the fresher's tag. The kind of growth that TCL has given you is difficult to achieve in any other company."

I pondered, replying in excitement, "Really, could you help my mother? I will be readily grateful to you."

J smilingly responded, "Anything for you, baby! Sweetheart, heartbeat, beloved. You have no idea how much I love you. I cross my heart and hope to die!"

"But, how soon can we get a job for mom?" I questioned with eccentricity.

He replied with ease, "Just leave it on me. I shall take care of everything. You just focus on me. And promise me that you will never leave me."

I said, "Yes, I won't leave you. Thank you for helping me out".

I had almost forgotten everything. J had given me a reason for happiness. I forgot my scheduled interviews, kept on talking to J and reached home with sweets. Suspicious about the glow on my face, mom probed, "What makes you so happy today? I was dying to see this smile on your face."

I hugged mom and said, "I got a surprise for you. I will reveal it soon. But, stay assured that we can be at peace now. Our days of melancholy are finally over. Time to cheer up."

Mother knew I had been working hard to cope with the drowning economy of the house. I was kissing up after each make-up with J, for I knew J is working towards solving my problem. The routine continued, but the visuals of a smile back on mom's face kept me driving. I was breathing with J for mom. Time passed by, and a month passed without any fights. I had almost learnt the ropes of staying with J when Shahid called after a very long time. J was not keeping well that day. He was on a call and said, "I will be completely alright if I see you. That's why I am coming to the office. Keep a firm hold on the team, and if anyone approaches you, just buzz him/her off. Rest, I am on my way." J hung up after saying this. I had kept the cell on the desk to check through the mails when the phone rang again. I picked up, reading through the e-mails, speaking, "Please, get ready. Let me work too."Shahid replied, "Pooja, it's me. Shahid."I bit my tongue and shouted ouch.

Sahid replied, "Are you ok?"

I spoke, "Yes...Yes...Yes, I am wonderful. I am, I am sorry I confused you with J."

"J? Who's J?" Shahid asked.

I replied, "My manager, Jeeva."

"Oh, but it didn't sound like you were talking to your manager. Nevertheless! I am visiting India for 15 days, shall I bring something for you?" he questioned.

I said, "No, everything is ok."

"Oh, by the way, how's aunty doing and how's her job?" he asked.

I was silent for a minute.

"Hello, hello, what happened?" asked Shahid in concern.

"Well, mom lost the job to a molester," I whispered.

"What? Seriously, I need to see you both. You don't even mention a thing, Pooja. I am very disappointed. Am I not your friend?" he questioned.

I said, "You come soon. We will sit at home and talk."

I had disconnected the phone and found J standing behind my chair.

"What was Shahid saying?" he interrogated angrily.

I said, "Nothing."

He repeated, "You liar. Tell me, what did Shahid say?"

"He just said that he will come to India and meet us," I politely replied.

He probed, "When?"

I replied, "I don't know. He didn't mention the dates."

I lied to him about this because I knew he would create havoc.

He said, "I know you are lying to me. You liar, you cheat. You keep on ditching me. I gave you my entire 10 months. You have killed the trust factor. You rapist."

He walked to his cabin with such colossal accusations. I wanted to explain, but he wasn't ready to understand. The daily chores were in pace while we wrapped up everything at 5:00 PM. The hegemony prevailed in the entire team as J grew louder in admonishing his reporters. While making an exit, he commanded me to go home in his car. I agreed. We sat in his car in the parking lot and left the office.

"I have finally found someone who is ready to help your mom in getting a position at one of the reputed private firms of India," J started.

"Really?" I questioned.

"Yes, I had circulated her CV at almost every organisation. Since the influence of her ex-director is pretty persistent, few of the organizations denied any job, but most of them accepted the CV for the second round," he said.

I replied with a flat face, "Yeah, it's almost 1.2 months since CVs have been floated but no luck yet."

He took a deep breath and said, "Don't worry! I got this. But what shall I get in return?"

"I am sorry," I stumbled.

"I mean, you should travel with me for this to Jaipur to celebrate your mother's new job," he advised. I scowled and didn't reply.

He looked at me and spoke, "I have been doing so much for your mother, and you can't even do this. Bad, Pooja. Come on, we will have fun."

I just nodded in acceptance, thinking that at this point in time, it is indispensable to plan for a vacation. I didn't utter a word. We reached home, and he kissed my lips, bidding me goodbye.

A sad, sullen face reached home, mother asked, "What keeps you tensed every day?"

I just smiled replying, "Just a long day, ma."

I was seeking help for my mother and I. Love for J was turning rebellious. There was a time when a lot of guys in the office used to hover around me. Few in flirtatious spirit, some in a peaceful mind. Today, no one wants to even talk to me. I was a lonely soul in space. I was a star, which was dying every day. Days passed, followed by months, but nothing worked in my and mother's luck. It was not that J wasn't trying his best for mother, it was just that I had given up inside. It was J all around, just J.. Satakshi, at home, lived with the benefit of the doubt. Often, Satakshi questioned Jeeva for his little attention towards the family. She knew there was something which was keeping him off but she had no option than to stay quiet. The future of the kids was a gigantic wall between her, and the secretes Jeeva held.

Jeeva was shrewd enough to maintain his family, office and love life. He was content, happy and proud of the person he was. Finally, the day of Shahid's arrival came. Fortunately, that was Saturday, my week-off. Shahid travelled from the airport straight to my house. He met my mother and I, expressing his concern for my mother's lost job and my struggle in the office. Shahid assured some financial help, which we denied. But he was reluctant and keen on helping us. He said, "If not money, I shall get all the grains and food for the month through the online delivery system, and none of you will deny this."

"We don't want any help, my son. You just keep visiting us. It feels good. It's just Pooja, I have. It will be good to have another child," delivered mother.

Shahid broke into tears and hugged mother saying, "My mother expired while I was in Singapore, I just felt as if my mom was talking to me." My mother hugged him.

Three of us had a long chat over dinner. Shahid left late that evening, while J had already dropped 100 missed calls on my phone. Perhaps, keeping the phone at hands has been a new fashion, and that's why J was furious with me. As Shahid left, I called J asking, "What's wrong? There were guests at my home. Am I supposed to pick your call every time?"

J replied angrily, "Am I stupid here, waiting for you since evening. We spent just a lovely time back home. I was in those memories. What a shameless creature you are. You forget everything within the blink of an eye. You have to pick my call whenever I call, in any situation. If there are guests at home, you could have called me and informed by saying, 'J, there are some guests at home. You, please, don't be angry, I will call you once free'"

I politely replied, "J, I was not in a condition. Mother was with me."

Mother was standing behind the wall; however, she didn't mention this later in any conversations. Shahid visited us the other day too. We had a gala time together. It felt as if happiness has found its destination. Three of us went out for shopping, spending splendid moments of life. I had almost forgotten about J, office and the sufferings. Smiles, happiness, and peace here were unconditional, limitless and expected nothing in return. Unaware of the fact that J had been following us since morning, I didn't update J of my sneak out with Shahid. All he knew was that I was out with my mother. But he knew the truth and was burning in anger. The moment we returned home, he started dropping texts back to back which read:"You are a liar, a cheat.""Why didn't you tell me Shahid was with you?""You denied meeting and talking to him, why did you meet him?"

"Am I a bastard following you everywhere around? That's my love for you.""You always need new people around you. You are playing with my emotions.""Don't leave me, Pooja.""Just say once, you don't want me. I will walk out of your life. But I am telling you, I won't be able to live without you.""You are my lifeline, but, please, leave me, Pooja.""I can't see you like this with anyone else. No one in your life is allowed. It's just J. No Shahid. I cross my heart and hope to die""A bloody Muslim? These Muslims are heartless. You are doing wrong."I replied on the text, "J, please, calm down. It's nothing as you are perceiving. Trust me. We are friends. Since you don't like him, I don't talk about him to you. Please, try to understand. My love for you is real, but I have my limitations.""Then do one thing. Come downstairs and meet me," J replied on the text.

I replied, "Are you serious? It's 12:00 AM. I can't come downstairs. My mother is up."He returned the text, "If you love me, today, you will come downstairs. If anything happens to me today, you will be responsible."I started weeping in stress. Mother knew something was not right.

She came to me and asked, "Tell me honestly, what's wrong?"

I cried and spoke, "Nothing, mom. Just worried about you and the situation at home. My efforts in getting another job for myself are in vain. I have to work here till I get a new one."

Mother hugged me and said, "I am sure, none of the problems you mentioned is big enough to put you in such distress. There is definitely something which you are not sharing. It's fine if you don't want to. But, let me tell you, I will find it out. The day I find out the person behind your stressful tears, I am gonna tear him into pieces."

Mom's hug was a relief. I felt empowered, and I didn't reply to any of J's text further. The phone kept ringing but in silent mode. Mom cuddled me and carried me like a baby to sleep. That day, for the first time, I had the most peaceful sleep. It felt that I wasn't sleeping for a year, and now somebody has come to my rescue. Later, the next day, when I left for the office, mom discussed the problem with Shahid. Shahid in discussion with mom said, "I don't know aunty, but Pooja looked really upset even on the day I left for Singapore. Something is troubling her. She is fighting inside against something. At the same time, she is pretending to be courageous. I wanted to talk about this to her but hesitated as I am not sure what opinion she has of me." Mother discussed the grave matter with Shahid, and both of them concluded that they would investigate this matter. I knew the day in office won't be peaceful, for I had ignored J's calls and messages. I was worried about going to the office but had to. It was a thumb rule to dial J once I de-board the cab and to stay on the call with him till the moment I reach home. He didn't want me to entertain anyone except for him. As a routine, I called J. J picked the call and said, "So, finally, the shameless creature has called. Do you know where I was last night? What all I suffered in your name? You bloody ignored my messages. How dare you leave me for hours, for 12 hours! I left my family, my wife, my kids just to be with you. You are a heartless human being. Pooja doesn't love J. Pooja is a selfish bitch."

I wept on the phone saying, "Please, don't say that. I didn't ignore you. You were misbehaving.

I have all the rights to spend time with my family. You were at the peak of your anger for off beam reasons. Please, be a little soft on me. Please."

J denied and kept on rebuking me for my evening's behaviour. In extreme fear of being assaulted more by J, I left the office, barefoot, walking for miles. I turned off the phone. I just wanted to die today, to get rid of my problems. Maybe I wasn't mature enough. But that was the truth. I kept on walking, while the clock turned the directions. My body had started dehydrating. I was hungry, but I ignored my body calls. J grew concerned about me and kept on calling on the switched-off cell. From morning to afternoon and afternoon to morning, people at the office were clueless. Almost every one of them was searching for me; Sakshi in the nearby park, Manu near the red light, Sudhanshu sir near the cab station.

It seemed like the TCL R&D team was on a different search expedition. People had given up when Rakhi had an idea, "Pooja could have gone home as well." J, in no time, called my mom and asked, "Is Pooja home?"

Mom frowned and freckled. She said, "She is at the office. Who are you?"

J replied, "I am Jeeva Singhal, her manager."

"What's wrong with my daughter?" mother enquired.

He replied, "Ma'am, we can't find Pooja anywhere in the office. I don't know where she has gone. I mean she came to office, but suddenly disappeared."

"Suddenly disappeared! Do you even know, what are you talking Mr. Jeeva?" mother shouted. "If anything happens to my daughter, I shall sue you, I am telling you." Mom disconnected with such daunting words.

She immediately called Shahid and explained the situation. Shahid, in no time, reached home, letting off the steam against TCL company. Both mom and Shahid were leaving when they saw me at the apartment gate. I was barefoot with a carry bag in the most broken state. Mother shouted, "Pooja." Hearing her, I fell unconscious on the ground. Shahid and mom helped me to my room and called a doctor.

Meanwhile, mother called Jeeva saying, "Pooja is home in an appalling state. What did you do to my daughter?" J was big-time scared that I would say something against him. He replied, "I am coming," banging the phone. He drove furiously to reach me before I woke up. But the doctor arrived before him. After careful examination, he told Shahid and mom, "Pooja, has been empty stomach since morning. It's stress and exertion, which led to this unconscious state. I have given her an injection. Once she gets up, please, ask her to eat something energetic. For any issues, you can call me." Shahid accompanied the doctor downstairs saying to my mom, "My sisters are alone at home. I shall take your leave now. For any issues, do call me." Mother thanked both Shahid and the doctor for such ready help. I too woke up.

Mom was sitting beside me. She hugged me tightly saying, "What would have I done without you. What made you leave the office? Tell me. Let the genie out of the bottle."

I was about to utter 'J....' but Jeva arrived interrupting, "Pooja, How are you? What's wrong? Where did you go? I was in a meeting when you left. Please, tell me what was bothering you?" Mom rose up to get J a glass of water; ad interim, J stared in my eyes, requesting me not to speak anything in front of mom.

Mom returned with a glass of water. J faced mom saying, "I am giving this girl an off for 4 days. Aunty, please, take good care of her and bring back the most efficient employee of my team." Mom giggled and asked Jeeva to leave so that I could take rest. J agreed and left the house. Mom hugged me, fetched me some dinner, kissed my forehead and helped me sleep. I didn't say anything to mom. I didn't want her to be worried about me, but a mother is always aware of her child. One should never forget that, not even the child itself. Mom cheered me up the next morning asking, "How's my lovely baby child doing?" I smiled in real happiness. It felt like I was a 1-year-old kid, who would smile at everything its mother says. Infanthood was back. Mom hugged me tightly, and kissed my cheeks nearly 100 times. I thoroughly enjoyed it.

I wanted to get back into her womb again and restart everything from scratch. How I wish things would have been like a toy of a 1-year-old kid, who always had someone around to bring back anything it throws. How I wish I wouldn't have been a girl, in a pathetic country like India. In spite of so many slogans, a girl remains a girl to a man. The man could be a father, a teacher, a brother, a lover, a friend or a jack of any profession. Being a woman according to the internet is, 'The **female** pelvis is wider than the male, the hips are generally broader, and **women** have significantly less facial and other body hair. On average, **women** are shorter and less muscular than men.' But, it should be, 'The female responsibility is wider than the male, the assaults are generally broader, and women have significantly less spatial and more body despair. On average, women are weaker and less popular than men.' The pen cap rolling in mouth, I jotted a dedication to millions out there struggling, which read as:She taught, the sky is an endless shelter,

She was happy, at least one thing is for free,

One beautiful day, a storm began to melt her,

She sought help, begging, "find me!"

Tossed by the storm, she pushed hard,

Like a sailor, fighting the wind of the sea,

Struggling on, with body and soul marred,

She sought strength, gruntling, "Find me!".

Washed away by winds and water,

She launched on his hands, which had a fee,

His eyes were lit by passion, of slaughter,

She ought to rescue, chiding, "Find me!"

Fluttering like a bird in a cage,

She now had to take his permission to pee,

All-day fighting a nervous inside rage,

She revolted atrocities, shouting, "Find me!"

Hours, days, months, and years passed,

The storm felt a lot better than he,

Losing all hopes, she died in the dark at last,

She fought bravely, screaming, "Never find me!"The phone rang. It was J. I answered the call. "Hello, Pooja, my life. How are you?" asked Jeeva.

I cleared my throat and spoke, "I am fine, thank you. How are you?"

He replied, "I am fine. Where were you yesterday? I was so worried. Did you call Shahid, your friend and partied with him yesterday?"

I gulped up my anger and started shivering. After a long pause, J again spoke, "Never mind. You are ok now, right? You nearly killed me. The entire team was on search an expedition yesterday. I have assured your mother that nothing like this will happen again. So, please, I insist, don't run away from fights. Face them. You could have talked to me, explained the situation. You know, your J. Where shall I go without you? You are my everything. I cross my heart and hope to die." I, in a quivering voice, uttered, "I am fine now." J understood that I was still upset with yesterday's conversation. He handled the situation saying, "I have finally got the call for your mother's job." I didn't repeat anything. "Oh, you aren't happy this time?" he questioned.

I plainly replied, "She has been getting this job since last 4 months. I have given up on you totally for this. It's mom's fate now. We will manage. Thank you for all your help."

He frowned and shouted, "I have left no stone unturned to get this offer letter. Don't act foolishly. I am coming to your home with the offer letter."

CHAPTER 13
SMILE- YOU ARE IN POSSESSION

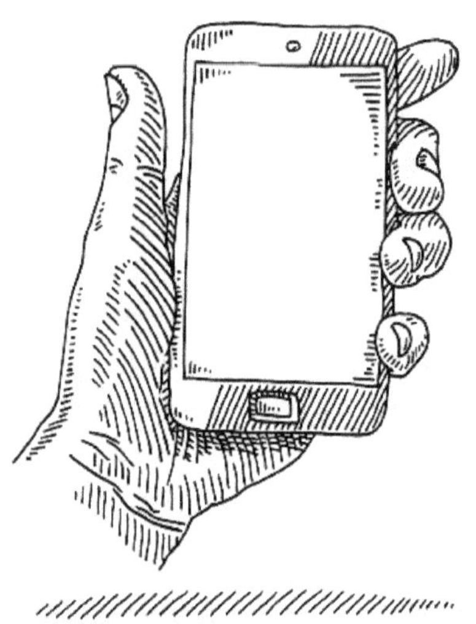

Jeeva was smart enough to call from the parking lot of my apartment. He ensured that I was at home, watching out and guarding my house, especially on weekends. This way, he made sure that no one gets inside or walks inside. He rang the doorbell right after 10 minutes after the call got disconnected. I was taking a shower. Mom opened the door. He wished morning to mom, while mom asked him to take a seat. He cleverly asked, "Where is Pooja?"

Mom innocently replied, "Pooja is taking a shower." He shook his head in regard and asked for a glass of water. Mom brought him water. He then showed her the offer letter, congratulating her on the new job. A smile appeared on my mother's face as if she found her lost dream back. "How did you get this? I never applied in this company," mother questioned. Jeeva smiled and replied, "I had been trying very hard to get this for you. Finally, I got it. I got your old salary matched too. Now you can also work and support Pooja. The only demerit is that you will also have to attend the office on Saturdays." Mother got a little worried.

Jeeva asked the reason behind that. She replied, "Pooja stays upset these days, I can't leave her alone like this every Saturday." Jeeva caught hold of the moment and smartly replied, "Don't worry. I shall babysit her on Saturdays. I am always at your service." Unaware of his presence at home, I walked out of the washroom in a towel. Jeeva totally enjoyed the show winking at me but pretended to mom as he didn't see anything. One thing was worth appreciating about Jeeva, was he was a keen observer and a quick action owner. People could be easily fooled by him. I got ready and walked outside.

"Hello, Sir," I greeted Jeeva.

J replied, "Hello, Madam. How are you? Congratulations, finally, your mom got the offer." The first thing which came to my mind was the Jaipur trip, which I promised in return.

For a while, I was clueless and lost. Mother held my hand and asked, "Aren't you happy, Pooja?"

I replied fumbling, "Haap... Happy, very happy. This calls for a celebration."

I knew the lion's share of happiness belongs to the 42-year-old gentleman.

"Both of you sit and talk. I shall get back from a society meeting," mom walked out of the home, saying this. J was staring at me in the most romantic way ever. His eyes said it all.

He uttered, "So, finally, Jaipur trip. Bookings have been made. Our hotel is a 4-star property. You will love it. Sorry to say Pooja, but I didn't have money for this trip. Somehow, I have been under so much loan pressure these days. But don't worry, I broke Ashna's piggy bank to arrange for our travel."

"Really? What kind of father are you? You broke your daughter's saving for your enjoyment?" I questioned.

He asked me to shut my mouth. Jeeva said, "Anything to be with you. I can sell my entire property just to spend 5 minutes with you. See, only to go on this trip, I worked hard for months. The fruit of hard work is always sweet. I never worked hard in my student life, but yes, today, I feel I have done something. So pack up, we are leaving tomorrow. I have already sanctioned you the leaves, I will also manage mine. Let's bash Thursday, Friday, Saturday and Sunday."

I replied, "What would I say to mom?"

He scoffed and said, "I have taken care of that, let's get going. I am excited to babysit you every Saturday, kissing you all over, squeezing you in my arms. Feeling your breath, touching you everywhere, and caressing your breasts. Oh my God! I am growing crazy just at the thought of it." I was numb, thinking is it love? If it is love, why does it sound selfish? Why aren't my wishes and consents asked for? Yes, I love you too. But my love is losing cannons, and yours are living under the rock.

Mother returned, and Jeeva asked to take our leave. I walked Jeeva downstairs since he insisted for some official discussion. He reminded me, "I have told mom about our office work. I will draft another email like last time. Show that to her, so that she loses the actual thread of our travel. I love you." I just said, "Ok." He left, and I returned home. I addressed mom, "Mom, I am very happy for you. Let's celebrate."

Mom replied, "You have to leave for your office trip tomorrow. Jeeva informed me a couple minutes back. Will celebrate once you are back."I nodded and walked inside my room. I started packing. J was mad as a box of soapy fogs. I was turning crazy as a hatter. The nudnik was waiting outside the apartment sharp at 8:00 AM, honking, texting and calling to come soon. I hurried up and got late by 12 minutes. "Next time you come late, I shall leave you behind," J warned me. The journey started. Jeeva hugged me while driving, resting my head on his shoulder. "Baby, I am thrilled to travel. I am so excited. We will hop at all the places, all the forts, and all the amazing places there. Hold my hand baby, tight," J screamed in excitement. I picked up my phone to play some South Indian songs when my phone rang. It was Shahid. I looked at J, while the phone kept on ringing. J asked me to take the call. I said, "It's okay if I don't take the call." He grew angry and asked me to take the call.

I picked it up, saying, "Hi Shahid, How are you?" Shahid replied, "I am fine, Pooja, How are you? I am sorry I didn't get time to meet you before leaving. But I am coming back again. This time, with a lot of surprises for you."

I smiled saying, "Thank you, Shahid. I am glad I mean so much to you. I will be waiting for you," and I hung up. J, as usual, made a sullen, long face. I apologised to J. J talked only on one condition. I asked, "What?"

He riposted, "You have to swear on me that you will stop talking to him forever. So, now you have to choose between Shahid and me."

"You are just making your mark, J," I screamed. "This is beyond bearing."

J smiled and said, "Choice is yours!"

We were quiet for a very long time after this heated conversation. He was marching on the beat of his own drum. He pulled over the car for refreshments saying, "You can use the toilet and tell me what you wish to eat." I walked out of the car, straight into the washroom. I broke into tears. I very much wanted to call mom but didn't. I knew mom would be worried. I, then, walked out of the washroom with a bright face. J and I sat in a restaurant, grabbed a burger and left again for the journey. He disturbed the silence by saying, "Hand over your cell phone."

I said, "What?"

"You heard me right. The cell phone, please," he requested. I handed over the phone to him. He scrolled through all the chats, emails and gallery ensuring I am not in love with anyone else apart from him. He, then, activated the location service on the phone, sharing my live location with him. He explained, "Every time, you walk out of the house, you have to share your live site with me. I am saying this because now mom is working and I have to take good care of you.". He handed over the phone back to me. I innocently received the phone with a cloud of thoughts raining in my mind. I had to spend a month of Sundays with J on the trip. Our return was scheduled on Sunday early morning. We reached the hotel, submitted our IDs' and finally, made ourselves comfortable in the room. J grew romantic the moment we entered the house. I was watching the pool from the window side, when he hugged me from behind, holding me tight, kissing my neck and cheeks. "I am so happy, baby. You are with me. This is the best moment of my life." He then turned me towards him, kissing my lips. The heat was now too much. He rested me against the wall, kissing me desperately. He started removing my clothes, first by pulling over my T-shirt. He jerked the T-shirt up and threw it on the floor. Dancing his tongue over my face, J started licking me. I started moaning in excitement. By the time he reached my navel, I realised that I was totally naked. He asked me to spread my legs and inserted his legs in between. He held his arms across my breasts and suddenly, the doorbell rang.

He stopped kissing me and screamed, "What the hell?" He pushed me into the washroom, handing over my clothes and walked to the door with a bare chest and fitted jeans. He scolded the room service for interrupting in between. The housekeeper apologised and handed over the heavy luggage to J with some complimentary water bottles. We had left our luggage downstairs. J knocked the washroom, hinting that the pass is clean. I walked out of the restroom, fully dressed. He exclaimed, "Come on, who asked you to dress up. I had to play more." I sat close to him, resting my head on his shoulder. We then decided to have lunch and catch up on the forts before they close. After lunch, we drove through the city, visiting places, clicking pictures, tasting the food around. My senses grew enthralled with forts and ancient sites. My mood lifted, and I was now enjoying the old, mystic places including the Bhangarh fort (Declared haunted by the ASI), Briraj Bhawan Palace and many more. The feeling of being a part of this place at some point in time was intense. At the end of time, I was almost convinced that I was the deceased princess of Bhangarh. Fun was leaping my way. J would always extend his hand, telling me, "Either my way or the highway," which I totally ignored. On the way back to the hotel at 11:00 PM, J pulled over. He stepped out of the car and walked to my door. He pulled open it and started kissing my lips. In the dark night, it was just J and I on the outskirts of the city. J was losing hold of his cock, which was growing tight, on the brink of the blast. He pulled back my seat and started kissing me wildly. My touch acted as an astringent to him. I loved him too, but didn't feel it right to act childish in the middle of the road, in the middle of the night. I stopped him saying, "J.. J.. J.. stop. This is a road. We can be attacked by anyone, dacoits, police. Please, let's get back to the hotel."J proposed, "Only on one condition." I asked, "What?"

He said, "You have to dance for me in a bikini."

To get out of the situation, I nodded in agreement. I pulled back my seat, and we drove back to the hotel. Back in the room, J had ordered the food of his choice with light music in the background. The food had arrived, and I was all dressed up to dance. We ate and danced like we were in the neck of the wood. The night stayed young, we were all naked lying on the bed draped in the payers of the blanket. J was biting my ears. I was half asleep. J wasn't letting me sleep saying, "I am not here to sleep, so I won't let you sleep either. Come on, get up, let's dance on the tunes of love." I was almost dead sleep, not knowing what's happening around. For two days, the events were on repeat, we would make love, eat, dance and visit monuments and historical places. The journey had almost come to an end. In the meantime, J ensured checking my phones, updating about his wellness at home and making me talk to my mom at a regular interval of 5 hours to keep her updated about the critical work happening at the office. The three-day trip finally came to a halt. I was carrying back certain warnings, some freshness from the historical places and some pains at places of the body which can't be understood. The routine life of staying on call started from the moment I de-boarded the cab, till the time I shut my eyes. J's interference at my home was quite regular now. Most of the times, mom didn't stay home, so he started using it at his advantage. J pro-actively started working from my home, where he would work less and eat me more. The physical addiction grew stronger day by day. I was 24, much adult than a teenager, but still unable to break this monotony of life. My nine-to-five-job was restricted to keep J happy and abide by whatever he asks. This would benefit my physical health, my psychological health, my job, and my mom's job. To all the intents and purposes, I was dependent on me, featured as an independent lady of the 21st century. I had now become a victim of depression and anxiety. Breathing issues and restlessness were new unwanted guests of my life. At times, when mom planned her official tours, J would stay at my place. He would visit his home for smaller periods, ensuring I don't leave the house, checking my live location updates. I was trapped inside my own house. Usually, food was ordered from outside, at times I used to cook it. The office was well-taken care of by J. My creativity was dying inside. Pen and papers hated me for the kind of person I had turned into. In one place or the other, I hated myself too. Practically, J and I never had proper sex, not that I was riding his ship, but couldn't even deny that I had surrendered to him. It was kind of him that he never brutally forced me for sex, but he had this great hypnotising and controlling power because of which, he never had to do anything. For another 1 year, the love of odds stayed in fashion with no names and no pack drills. Fuming fights on not sharing the live locations with him or some hangouts with friends were regular. I had started deleting logs and messages to escape this torturous vigil. Eventually, the friends with whom I stayed connected started parting away, because J would barely allow me to talk or chat with them. He made me his world and expected the same in return. The connection between my colleagues and me broke long back. Shahid was the only hope, the only friend of mine, whose affection always comes without condition. Shahid never looked for my attention and always gave his best to my mother and me. Back in the subconscious mind, my love and respect for Shahid were unparallel and prodigious, irrespective of his favours to me. I knew that I don't love him because I had my commitments to J, but I knew I like him way beyond J. I would often ask my mother to define love. Mom would say,

"Daughter, I had this misconception that love is always sacrificing. But at this age, I realise it is also about sacrifices on your sacrifice. Love is not a possession or obsession. Love is divine. Love is also hatred in disguise. It can actually destroy you, but it will save you at the end, without expectations. Once it destroys you and changes the person you are, it no more stays love. It converts into hate. It's a misconception that love always wins. No, love only wins, when it has the power to do things better in the end. Love is an impersonator, which changes with your thoughts and actions. If priority grows wild, love turns into possessiveness. If trust crosses limits, love turns into a spy, if passion exceeds, love turns into a murderer."

A sense of confidence was injected back into me that I am not doing something wrong. I love J and my commitment was standstill. But what J was doing was undoubtedly way deviated from love. I was living in guilt of snatching away a father from two kids. Snubbing a wife, who has been committed to a man for the last 18 years. The conversation with my mother was a painkiller to my wound. J was busy with some relatives and friends; therefore, his calls were limited today. My imaginations were a rainbow, and I wanted to paint the pages with my colours. Shahid had also returned and visited us. We had a gala lunch, while I read one more of my composition. Since the lunch was served, I made the best use of the opportunity to rhyme up the love with food. I dedicated it to both Mom and Shahid gearing up in lemony love:Petty fights, fumes like a burning clove,

Cuddles, comfort like folded wings of a dove,

Patience and Perseverance requires of our behove,

Neither chilly nor sweet, ours is lemony love.

Crunchy little hearts swirling in soup,

Lips embark cold below and heat above,

Heat condenses and wiggles like rolling hoop,

Breaking the boredom of meticulous push and shove.

Our presence in each other is garlic with onion,

Savouring the taste buds like a velvet glove,

Squashing few juicy drops in grand canyon,

Titilates, the flavour, bridging gaps in neat wove.

Fingers run crazy on zesty special seasoning,

Melting the cheese of the busty cuisine,

A delicious silence lock lips all day and evening,

An extravagantly tangy love, the world has ever seen.

Our fingers paint in colourful sauces,

Marinating in the assorted creamy lust,

Slipping through and holding charges as bosses,

Neither savage nor extreme, our's is tipsy thrust.

Cooked or uncooked, our love stays fresh,

Like the steam of barbecue in heaven above,

The odour is alive in our sensual frame of flesh,

Tossing, Tangling, whirling and precipitating in lemony love.

The day ended. J called me late at 11:00 PM, saying, "I missed you so much. But it didn't feel like you missed me. No texts, no messages. What's going on? You didn't even share your location with me? Now tell me where you were roaming? Your number is on track and surveillance. I know you have been using other phone numbers to ditch me, but worry not. I got your back." Tears rolled down my cheeks. I said, "I was home only, that's why I didn't call back or share the location. You mentioned earlier that you will be surrounded by guests.""So what?" he screamed. "You know, I never miss any of your calls. I called you twice, and you didn't respond. How dare you didn't pick my call? What kind of love is this? For 24 hours, you didn't even drop a single text. I was dying in wait. You think I am a fool, you think it is a game. I have read all the texts you have been dropping to others, throughout the day, except me."

I broke into tears and started weeping. He hung up the phone, as mom asked me the reason behind my upset mood. I couldn't hold it this time and told her, "J has been misbehaving a lot with me these days, I don't know why. I am scared of his calls now." Mom asked, "Who's J? I am gonna kill that bastard. Who is scaring my daughter?" I replied, "Mr. Jeeva Singhal." Mother was in shock and asked me to sit in conference with her.

CHAPTER 14

MORAL MURALS OF MORONS

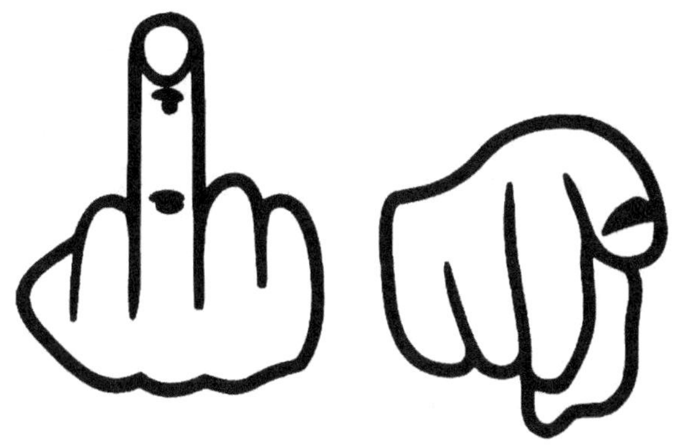

Mom asked, "What's going on? Explain in detail?" I didn't give an in-depth insight into the happenings in the past two years but gave a superficial idea. I told her that work has taken a toll on me. I should be switching. I was waiting for a better hold on the corporate experience, and it was high time to change. Mom repeated, "You are not telling me the precise reason. Still, I trust you. But I will find it out either by hook or crook." That night mom and I slept together, while the phone was ringing all night. J was getting irritated. He didn't sleep the entire night.

Early morning back to the office, the same routine started. But today, I made no calls to J. I reached office and dropped my resignation email, keeping the HR in CC. J was in a meeting, unaware of my deed. I packed up my bag in an hour, preparing to leave. I was in no mood of serving the notice period. Shahid was already in town. I called him to pick me up from the office. I was making an exit from the reception, when J screamed, "Pooja." I halted, turned back and replied, "Yes, Sir." J ran towards me, panting. "Please, take back your resignation," he commanded. I replied, "I won't take it back.""Pooja, I will slap you for this step of yours. I know you have no other offer with you."

"Now, there is no room to swing a cat. I have made my mind," I replied confidently.

"Does that mean you are leaving me? I know Shahid compelled you to do this?" he complained. I replied, "I am not leaving you because I have genuinely loved you. For your question, I trust Shahid more than you but that doesn't mean I love him. Rest you are smart." J was astonished at my confidence. He started weeping, asking me to stop. It was hard, but I walked out of the reception. J followed me, shouting, crying, "Pooja. Stop. Please, stay for me. Please, wait." He fell on my right foot, begging me to stay and take back the resignation. I melted. Perhaps, the firey love inside turned to be a snowy adulation. Even the office population was thin that day, so J managed to be a clown outside the office premises. "I promise to shut my mouth. I won't say anything to you. I won't throw sarcasm at you. Trust me, Pooja. I won't," he assured. I stopped, took a deep breath and returned to the office with J. I could see the love in his eyes and the guilt of treating me so harshly. I opened up my laptop and recalled the email, accepting that it slithered out of my drafts by mistake.

Things went in a silent box. J started behaving a little better than expected. No back to back calls for a change. I felt happy about myself that I took a call towards self-liberation. I was amateur in the prime time of love. Shahid, who came to pick me up, waited for almost an hour and then called me. I answered his call by saying, "Something urgent has come up. I am sorry. I won't be able to make it to home right now. Thank you for coming. I will catch you later in the evening." J knew it was Shahid calling, but he kept mum. That evening, I felt empowered. However, I was aware that J didn't like it. I am now his habit, and hence, he hushed the boils of anger. Mother also managed to get offs on Saturdays in her company. In fact, she had been approached by other companies for her excellent work. She will be making a switch soon, she informed me. Things were finally getting in control. J's babysitting, which was on a roll once was doomed. He was barely got a chance to visit my home or you can say that mom had found ways to spend more time with me.

Appreciations from other teams were falling like autumn leaves. For two years, I was on a wing and a prayer. J was on tenterhooks, as he barely talked to me. J's brains were on high alert. He was monitoring my hang-outs around with mom and Shahid. My mingling moments with the office colleagues and on the wagon parties with apartment girls,everything was watched on the down-low. None of it seemed to be in line with his expectations from me. He was planning a way out to get back in shape. Almost 2 years and counting, J for the first time, felt his importance is in the woods. He called mom, inviting her for a family get together. Mom didn't deny it but didn't even accept it readily. She said, "We shall try to be there for your anniversary." Later in the evening, after returning back from office, Mom informed me about the invitation. I passed the buck to mom and turned on the music. Mother turned off the music and said, "We will go." I agreed and said, "As you say, my lady."

I was returning back to my imaginative world, swirling in peaches and cream. Mother started talking about my marriage. "You are turning 25 now. It's high time to get married. So, what kind of guy is my daughter looking for?" I blushed and replied, "I am not gonna leave you by any chance. Anyone who has to get married to me will have to accept you too. I will take you in forced dowry." Mom burst into laughter, kissing my forehead. She said, "I have been talking to people and encountering a lot of proposals. Why don't you see some and tell me about your likes and dislikes?" I replied with a simple, "Ok." Shahid knocked the door saying, "May I come in gentle ladies." Mom and I said in sync, "Oh, please, come in" and we chuckled. Mom said to Shahid, "You have to assist me in writing something for Pooja." "I didn't understand aunty," Shahid said. I meant I am planning to find a suitable guy for Pooja. Can I expect your assistance in it? Since her father is not here, I will have to be both mother and father in her marriage." Shahid joined his hands in front of my mother and said, "I will work in the best of my ability aunty. Worry not." Mom went on to prepare the evening tea. Shahid asked me, "What are you doing this evening?" I replied, "We are invited at an anniversary party tonight. So we have planned to attend it. Why don't you join us?" Shahid chuckled, "No, thank you. Some other time." We had tea together, and then Shahid left. Mom and I got ready to attend the function. We boarded a cab and reached J's home. To our surprise, there was no party. Only we were invited. Mom met Satakshi (his wife), Ashna (his daughter) and Jahaan (his son), as J introduced them. I kissed the kids and presented them with the chocolates I had bought for them. J introduced me as Pooja and my mother as Pooja's mom to Satakshi. We had dinner together. Satakshi was a good-natured lady and friendship with her was a piece of cake. However, she treated me as a very junior employee of J. The chats were piping hot with food. Kids were enjoying a lot with me making puddle jumpers for fun. Followed by dinner, there was a dessert session, where kids enjoyed their favourite mouth-watering sweets. Out of the blue, mom started discussing her pipe dream of me getting married. J swallowed the saliva, hearing this. He played cat and mouse to change the topic, but mom was adamant. The subject didn't change. Mom hinted that he liked a boy whose name starts with 'S'.. I questioned mom, "You didn't mention this to me before." Mom replied, "I was about to tell you. The best part is that you have seen the guy as well and has pretty pennies." I kept on pondering but couldn't crack the riddle. J engaged mom in conversations, trying to get the name of the guy. He pulled out all the stops but failed since he tried imperiously. Mom said, "I will reveal the name once my daughter accepts the person. Otherwise, there is no point in spreading rumours." Everyone nodded in agreement. We thanked J and his family for organising a mammoth dinner and commemorating this day with us. We left for home. J couldn't control the powder keg and texted immediately, "Who is the guy?" I replied, "With a smiley, I don't know who is she talking about." J started, "I know you are lying. You liar. You cheat. I always knew there was something between you and Shahid. Why did you play with my emotions? You will get married to him. But you are mine. Will Pooja get married to a Muslim? Muslims are the worst creatures of this earth. Pooja, you will turn into a begum, hahaha........"

I replied, "Come on. You are moulding things into a different cast. There's nothing like that between Shahid and I. We are good friends. I seriously don't know who mom was talking about." J kept on accusing me of lying to him. He even claimed that there are physical relations between Shahid and I, which I rejected. J was trying to put a thumb on the scale, so I turned off the cell-phone. That was exasperating. We reached back home and slept peacefully.

J was deprived of sleep. That night, he drank heavily.

Satakshi asked, "Why are you drinking?"

He replied, "I am celebrating our anniversary. Why don't you join me?"

"I have to get up early with kids for their examinations. I am going to sleep," she replied in anger.

J kept on drinking and kept on calling me, texting me after every 5 minutes. "Please, talk to me. You are just mine, Pooja. You are mine. I shall kill Shahid, and then you will be mine forever." Early morning, I woke up at 6:00 AM, checked my phone and found 2 missed call and 100 texts from J. The content of the texts was rubbish and spoke about th same that was discussed last night. I didn't want to go to the office today. J would create more scene than ever, which would again root up my anxiety and stress level. I thought of dropping a leave application on email, but before that, J called and I picked it up, "Don't even think of not coming to the office. You have to reach the office and talk to me about yesterday. You have to confess that you are in real terms with Shahid. I won't leave you. If you don't come today, I will share negative feedback for your appraisal, and that would affect your ACR." I replied, "Calm down, I am coming." I took a shower, got ready and left for the office without breakfast. Mom was stunned to see that.

CHAPTER 15
HINDU-MUSLIM LOVE RIOTS

I reached the office. J was waiting for me, ready to listen to me and put that in his pipe and smoke it. Shahid was sitting back in his house, relaxed, watching television on the most disputed subject of years, 'Ram Mandir and Babri Masjid.' After the demolition of the Babri Masjid on 6th December 1992, the difference between Hindus and Muslims grew wider. Different Hindu and Muslim groups hold the opinions that the Ram-Janma Bhoomi belongs to them. The issue was sensitive. Shahid turned off the TV, bored of the same news everywhere. Petitions and pleas were submitted in the court to get the legal acquisition of the land. "When will people grow up? How does it matter even if it is a temple there? All gods are the same. Why do we divide humanity in the name of the religion? I don't understand," Shahid spoke to himself in disenchantment. I had entered the office, and I was fearful that J might kill me in anger today. Albeit, I knew he can't harm me, but his boiling blood scared the hell out of me.

I called Shahid before taking the lift. Shahid picked the call. I spoke, "Hi, Shahid. I thought since you will return in a week, let's catch up today in the evening. I will see you outside the office at 5:30 pm. And yes, if I don't pick up the phone, please check for me in the office."

Shahid replied, "That's ok. I shall come to pick you up, but why won't you pick up my call? And, why did you ask me to look for you in the office?"

"Nothing serious just joking," I giggled and dropped the call. The lift opened and J walked out of it, snatched my phone and asked me to follow him. I followed him in the elevator without uttering a word. He checked my phone, the last dialled one was to Shahid. I had anticipated he would cat amongst the pigeons once he sees the previous dialled call to Shahid. We sat in a meeting room, soundproof and locked.

"So, did you tell your lover that you have reached office?" J asked politely.

I replied softly, "You are misinterpreting J. I just called for a casual talk."

"Why didn't you call me? Don't you think you must keep me posted about your arrival at the office? And why didn't you share your live location on WhatsApp, even after repeated requests?" he questioned.

I started weeping. "Just shut your mouth. Weeping won't save you. I have all the call details of your number and Shahid's number. I know how frequently you two are talking. You tried to ditch me saying that you love me. Tell me what else is your plan? When are you two getting married?" he said angrily.

I sobbed and spoke, "Honestly, we are not getting married. There is nothing between us. We are just friends. Trust me, J."

"I know you didn't come here for love. You came here for your appraisal. Don't worry, I gave you a 25% hike this time so that you can spend lavishly at your wedding and book a honeymoon suite. You are a cheater, a liar, you played with my emotions," he said.

I kept on repeating, "None of it is true. I have quaked in my boots, so I called Shahid out of fear that you will harm me in anger," I replied.

"Oh, really? Then call him again and talk to him in front of me," he screamed.

I said, "Why should I talk to him in front of you? To prove what? What will I tell him, why am I calling him? Are you crazy?""Stop screaming and stop creating scenes in the office. I also know you have lodged a complaint against me in the office. You are trying to act smart with me. You will have to pay the price of your sins in this birth itself, my darling. I want to see you paying the price. Why are you ruining my life? Tell me. I will walk out of your life, just say once. Just say once that you don't love me. Say!" J screamed again.

"I don't want to say anything. Even if you don't trust me. You don't," I begged.

"Today, we will meet Shahid together. You will introduce me to him as your best friend. I want to talk to him. Take me to him right now. I know your love won't like me with you but let's do it," he thundered.

"Mom would know. Mom treats him like a son. Please, don't do this. This will directly go to mom. She will hold the wrong opinion about you. Shahid doesn't believe in religion. Stop acting foolish. Please," I requested.

J quoted the unquote, "Bloody, Muslims! They want to marry our Hindu ladies and convert them. Bastards. I won't let you turn into a begum. By the way, what name have you chosen for yourself, Begum Faiza or Begum Hafsa? Tell me, what is it?"

I bled in tears. "J, please stop this. Please, I beseech. You are killing me!" I solicited.

"Hahaha... I am killing you, or you are killing me every second? You know how it feels after knowing that the person whom you love so much betrays you, deceits you? I won't curse you saying that you will suffer in return. But tell me the truth." J said.

Outside the ambience was quite sensitive. People were in the dispute of building a Ram Temple or building a Babri Masjid over the ancestral property of Lord Ram in Ayodhya, Uttar Pradesh. Hindu- Muslims of the corporate were also a little agitated about this. They were keeping a distance from each other to avoid any combat over the sensitive issue. Shahid went to my mom to meet her and get her some groceries. Mom appreciated his help and adored him for being an ideal son to her. Mom didn't go to the office today, asthere was some Ram-Pooja (Worshipping Lord Ram) at home. The worship finished well, she even distributed the prasad (end-product of the worship in terms of food) to Shahid, neighbours and security guards. Shahid told mom that he was going to Ghaziabad to get some visa-related papers from the court. Mom wished Shahid goodbye. Before leaving, Shahid requested her to allow me for an evening outing with Shahid. Mom gave her permission to Shahid with the advice of getting home as early as possible, maximum by 11:00 PM. Shahid agreed to it. He also told mom, "Pooja sounded dull today on the call. Did you guys have a fight?"

Mom replied, "Even she didn't have her breakfast. She never does that. I am quite worried." Shahid assured mom that everything is ok and he shall take care of any issues after talking to me today in the evening. The clock struck 3. I was still captured inside the meeting room. J handed over the laptop to me in the meeting room and asked me to work there while he attended some meetings in between. I wanted to break free of the place but was hapless. J returned at 3:30 PM with a bang. "My meetings are over. Pack your bag. We are going to meet Shahid," he ordered. I started begging, "Please, J, I beg you. I touch your feet. This will create commotion at the house. Mom will be disturbed. For God's sake!"

J started packing my laptop and zipped my bag. "Come on, follow me," he began torturing me.

I stood up and tread on the heels of J. J was racing against time. We reached the parking lot. He handed over the phone to me and asked me to dial Shahid. I telephoned Shahid as if I was on a gunpoint. The phone rang, but Shahid didn't pick. I took a deep breath of relief. "Please, don't raise hackles. He didn't pick up because he is busy," I shouted. J clutched my hair tight pulling my head back and said, "You will call him again after 5 minutes. Do as I say? Else you will repent. Today, either he lives or I live, else I will kill ourselves both. Enough of your shit, baby." He held my hair tight, so that I can't move, waiting for 5 minutes. The clock struck 4:15, but Shahid didn't call. J dialled the call this time, keeping the phone on the loudspeaker. I was falling short of breath with every ring. I wanted this call to be failed. I prayed for none of the calls to reach Shahid.

On the other hand, Shahid was busy with the advocates. He had left his phone in the car haphazardly. J was reading the tea leaves, saying, "I know you must have dropped a message to him from some other number you carry. That's why he is not picking the call. But for how long will he not pick the call? We will keep trying." J called his friend and enquired about the location of the number. Shahid was not picking the call perhaps his work with the advocate got a little stretched. The security of the place was increased generously as red flags were shown about the temple dispute. Administration of the country was trying to re-invent the wheel to sort out the differences between the two religions. Mom was watching the television. Most of the news channels were warning people to return home as there were high chances of mayhem. Mom called me first. The phone was with J. J picked the call. Putting it on the speaker, he asked me to talk to mom without shouting and screaming. He warned me if I tell anything to mom, he will create more problems for me. I abided by what he said and answered, "Hi mom."

Mom replied, "Hi, daughter. When are you returning back?"

I replied, "In the next 1 hour. Why, what happened?"

Mom said, "Well, nothing severe, but I would recommend, today, you don't travel by a cab. Since you have already called Shahid for the evening meeting, it would be better if you both come directly to home. It's just not safe outside."

J's smile was rotten to the core. I replied, "Ok, Mom. As you say."J disconnected the call. "Oh, that was your plan. Today is the date evening. Fantastic," said J sarcastically.

I replied, "It's not a date but a causal meeting since he will leave next week."

"I can see how worried you are for him," J smiled and said.

On the spur of the moment, J received a text message from his friend. It was a location update on Shahid's number. "Ghaziabad! He is in Ghaziabad. Let's meet your lover now," J shouted. With speed, J was rubbing in, "Shall we take flowers for your lover, after all, it's a date, darling?" Roads were all vacant. It felt as if soon a curfew will be imposed. We reached Ghaziabad court in almost 25 minutes. J stopped the car, and my phone rang. This was Shahid's call.

J laughed like a devil and answered the call. Shahid spoke, "I am so sorry, Pooja. I was inside the court, talking to my advocate for visa issues. These advocates are such bribe mongers. My cell phone was in the car. I am reaching your place. I won't take more than 20 minutes. Stay inside. I don't find the outside ambience friendly."

I replied scared, "Don't go anywhere, I am coming to you."

"Where… where are you? Why are you coming here?" Shahid asked in concern.

J snatched the phone and spoke, "Pooja is with me. I brought her here. She is mine. Don't even think to come close to her, or else I will kill you."Shahid, in panicked voice, said, "Pooja… Pooja… Hello, who is this? Have you been kidnapped, Pooja? Who is this guy? Talk to me, Pooja? Are you listening to me?"

I started weeping. J continued, "What Pooja, Pooja? You hypnotise our Hindu women and get married to them to convert them. I won't let this happen."

Shahid replied, "Who are you, bastard? Tell me your name. I will kill you wherever you are. You dare not touch Pooja."

"I can feel your love for Pooja, my dear. But first tell me, who is Pooja to you?" questioned J, while I shouted, "Shahid, doesn't listen to him.

Please, hang on. I will be fine."

J replied, "She is my everything; my love, my life and I can do anything for her. Who the bastard are you?" J laughed like a devil again. "I knew both of you were in a relationship. It is proved today. His words and body language, everything proves it, Pooja. Now, what do you have to say? Go to your lover and leave me forever."

Shahid screaming on the other side, "What is this bastard saying? Are you with this person? Did you tell aunty? Pooja, where are you? Did he touch you? Answer me."

J pushed me out of the car, opening the door and spoke on the phone, "Here, I am sending your soulmate."

Shahid turned back, screaming, "Pooja, Pooja, I will solve everything. Come to me."I was walking in a confused state when J shouted from behind, "This Muslim guy has confiscated this girl. Our Hindu girl, Pooja. Catch the guy. He marries our innocent Hindu girls and convertthem into Muslims. This is love Jehad. Kill the bastard." Almost the entire mob got incited. J instigated violence amongst the Hindu crowd. The court premises, within no time, converted into a battlefield. Shahid escaped the Hindu mob, holding me in his arms. We entered the car. I had fainted in exertion. He drove safely home, handing me over to mom carefully. Mom panicked and started weeping on seeing me like that.

Shahid assured mom that he will tell her everything, till then, she has to be strong. He told her, "I have to go home and check on my sisters. Turn on the news channels, there has been a severe riot in Ghaziabad. Hindu and Muslims are killing each other."

Shahid left for his home. J was worried about me but was happy that finally, he could take Shahid on the trial of love. He saw Shahid running, which made him think that he was scared and hence, left the place. J was searching for me. He drove for almost 7-8 km to find me, but didn't see me. He was going nuts. He started calling people in the office, but nobody gave any positive response. Finally, after losing all the hopes, J called mom. Mom picked up the phone, "Aunty, Where is Pooja? Did she reach home? She was with me, then, suddenly, the riots started. I don't know, she got out of the car to get some medicines and then I lost her. Please, I am worried. Tell me once she reaches home." Mom didn't utter a word and J disconnected. Somewhere, she could connect the dots which didn't approve of J's innocence. Mom knew somewhere that he was lying to her. Mom waited for Shahid to return to understand the situation. My condition was critical.

The doctor visited home and asked mom to let me sleep after giving me a sleeping injection. Mom prayed all evening. The riots finally settled. News channels were full of headlines related to the riots. Ministers, administrators, leaders, shepherds, everyone expressed their concerns over such communalism and prayed for the souls of the martyrs. Nearly, 10,000 people died in the riots. Emergency and President's rule was imposed in Delhi NCR. Police were investigating the reason behind the riots. J managed to escape the cops since no CCTVs were installed at the place. J was nearly underground. He took leave for a week and moved out with his family to Meerut. He called mom again, asking, "Did Pooja return?"

Mom replied soberly, "Yes, and she is fine."

J said, "Aunty, somebody in my family is not well; therefore, I am leaving with my family for a week."

Mom replied, "Hmm..." J hung the call.

Next day, I woke up early morning. Schools, colleges, offices, private firms, everything was closed. I hurried to take a shower and got ready for the office. Mom was cooking breakfast. I hugged her and said, "Mom, I am leaving for office."

Mom scolded me and shouted, "Are you crazy? Do you even know what your condition was when Shahid brought you home? You better get married to a decent and pertinent guy. I will attain Nirvana then."

I consoled her, saying, "Why? What happened? Why are you saying like that? I am not getting married now. I have to take care of you."

Mom shifted the breakfast plate in front of me and probed, "What happened yesterday? Brief me up and please, don't lie. I have called Shahid as well.""Mom, I have to go to the office. I will talk to you in the evening," I ignored and stoop up.

"Sit down. Your office is closed today. There have been riots in Ghaziabad for almost 4-5 hours. Around 10,000 people died. Do you have any idea what's going outside?"

I fell back in the chair in a shocking state. "Where were you in the evening?" mom questioned, and Shahid knocked on the door.

Mom opened the door and asked Shahid to join us for the breakfast.

"Pooja, How are you?" Shahid asked. I couldn't stare back into his eyes.

I replied, "I am feeling better". We all sat as if we were in a round table conference, talking on a very profound and sensitive issue. Shahid asked me, "After I picked you up from the office, how did you fall off? I mean, you were absolutely well. You just stepped out to buy chocolate, and you fell."

I gave a 'What the fuck' look to Shahid, thinking what is he saying. Shahid said this purposely so that I look at him. He winked at me, and I understood that he will lie to my mom about yesterday to save me. His facial expressions clearly asked for help in the lie he was creating. "Tell Pooja, how did you fall?"

"Yeah, but I ate properly in the afternoon. I don't know how. And, mom told about the riots early morning. How did that happen?" I said

"Yeah, even I don't know. There were some notorious elements of the Hindu and the Muslim communities. Common citizens didn't do anything," Shahid added.

"That's what the police are saying," mom replied after watching the news.

Mom didn't mention about J's call to her but looked suspicious about our discussion, as if we are hiding something.

CHAPTER 16
IT WAS ALL ABOUT A WOMAN'S LOVE

Shahid left after breakfast. The situation was intense, so we didn't walk out of the house. Mom was not behaving the way she used to. Something was different about her, but I wasn't sure what because I was unconscious the time when the significant incidents occurred. 'Does mom know something?' This question was eating me inside? I was worried, but couldn't express.

Everyone was living in stress. I was thinking about J. What would have happened? He must have left me. I will lose everything. I was scared if he would expel mom from her job in anger. What Shahid must have been thinking about me? That 5-minutes long conversation between J and Shahid grew abusive. Both would have made substandard thoughts about me. I am doomed now.

I could barely work. I tried sleeping for some time but kept on changing the directions. It seemed as if the entire world has collapsed in a nuclear war. Mom was observing me every second.

I wanted to call J but was scared. What would happen if he didn't pick? What if he abused me? What if mom comes to know about what's going on? Whatever I do, it would turn against me. I was running in a tight ship. I left everything and sat in front of the TV. In some videos made by people on their phones, I saw a glimpse of me trapped near J's car. Sceptical about mom's mood, I changed the channel and walked back to my room. Shahid called. I picked his call and sneaked into the washroom. "Hello, yes? Shahid?"

"Pooja, I wish to know who that man was. He sounded more like a middle-aged person. Please, tell me did he hurt you?" he asked softly.

I was abashed by his thoughts. J spoke in an abusive manner, claiming that I belong to him, but he didn't even ask me. Why did he say so? Shahid had a different level of trust on me that I cannot do anything to hurt the integrity of my family. The faith he showed in me was explicitly different and divine.

I replied, "That man was J." And the phone got disconnected. I tried to call him back, but the network was jeopardised. It was done to stop the spread of inciteful messages and the possibility of any more riots in the city. I guess Shahid heard it, but how would he contemplate who J is? I tried reaching Shahid, but I was running in a buzz. With the end of the day, mom was running out of steam. She fell asleep right after lunch. I also laid on the bed, thinking about the entire episode. The doorbell rang, interrupting the deep silence. I got up and ran to open the door. The washer man had come to collect the clothes. I handed over a few outfits to him for ironing and he handed over a note to me. I was stunned. I opened it up and looked at the washer man. He had vanished. I got inside and carried the bill into the room so that mom doesn't wake up. The note read,

"Meet me tomorrow at the Holiday Inn and Suites— room no. 234, sharp at 4:30 PM.

J"

I hid the note under the mattress. Terrified and confused, I didn't know what to do. I wanted to go and explain things to J. I also didn't want to go because I knew that he will misbehave. But it was mandatory to go because I wanted to know what conversation he had with mom. I was more worried about what he must be thinking of me. I never lied to mom about anything. This was the first time I did. This was a significant issue. I finally decided to meet J and get into the depth of the situation. Forget about love, it's about the trust mom has on me, which seemed to be shattered. Later in the evening, the news headlines flashed 'Situation under control now. Schools, colleges and offices can resume without any fear from tomorrow. Govt. apologises to all those who suffered. The victims hurt and dead will be given a compensation of 1 lakh and 2.5 lakhs respectively.' Mom immediately questioned, "So, are you going to the office?"

I stammered and replied, "Yeah, yeah. If J… I mean Jeeva sir asks me to come, I will go." Mom said, "You work for J, Jeeva Sir, or you work for TCL?"

I hugged mom and said, "I work only for my mom to give her every happiness in the world and see her smiling every 5 minutes."

"Ok, ok. Stop buttering me. If you are going tomorrow, tell me, because I am not going tomorrow. I will have to prepare lunch for you," mom said.

"But why aren't you going?" I asked.

Mom replied loudly, "I am starting as the CTO in a news organisation. I got the offer letter day before."

"What? How? When? I mean, wow. Mom, you are genius," I expressed my happiness.

"But I am not happy," mom replied with a long face.

"Why, Mom?" I questioned inquisitively.

"Because my daughter has started hiding things from me," she replied.

I grew stressed. Freckles surrounded me like foam. I took a long pause.

Mom said, "What happened. I meant you got a raise of 25% and you didn't even tell me."

"Oh, yes. Raise. Yes, raise. I got it," I took a breath of relief.

"You should talk to me. I will save grace for you," mom advised. I agreed to what mom said. Mom added, "Let's celebrate once you are back from the office tomorrow."

I nodded and said, "Of course, mom."

I went to sleep. I had to finish some pending tasks. Neither mom nor I could sleep at night. I had issues, but what was the thing which was bothering mom? I had the most disturbing night of my life. Morning, 7:00 AM; both of us woke up together. Mom and I both got ready. We had breakfast together.

I asked mom, "Why are you getting ready? You said you won't go."

Mom smiled and said, "A mother's treasure and only best friend is her daughter. You are my sixth sense. You are my smile, laughter, worry, tears and satisfaction. I have a heart, but you are the heartbeat. You are my legacy. You gave me an identity and finally turned out to be my identity. My motherhood with you was less complicated and more rewarding. You are both my sun and my moon. I wake up every morning and look at you, thanking God for giving me a diamond. You shine every day, and then I safeguard you back into your case. You came to my life without a manual. It took me time to understand you, but you took no time to understand me. You have always been so mature. You never wept without any reasons. You never demanded anything. People say you always love your mother because you won't get another one. I mean, always love your daughter because you can't think of getting another. You have gifted me so many necklaces till date, you know which one is my favourite? It is when you hold your arms around my neck. I feel more beautiful in your embrace than in any outfit or jewellery. Being your mother, I must crush down every remorse that stands in your path. You are my extension. You are my biological road map, and I am your emotional road map."

There were tears in mom's eyes. She was welling up. I hugged her and cried out loud, "I love you, mom. I will always be your little girl, and you will be my treasure map, which I will keep on following, tearing away the critical paths because I don't want anyone closer to you than me. You know, I even feel jealous when you call Shahid 'kid'. You are only my mom. Ok? You belong to me. You are my proprietary, and I am yours. Today, I am brave, capable, pretty and can accomplish almost anything on this earth because you are my mother."

I stood up from the dining chair, to leave for the office. Mom said, "Stay, Pooja. Don't go. I don't want you to go today, please."

I said, "Mom, what's wrong? I am only going to the office. I will be back by the evening, then we will have ice-cream, noodles, and we will celebrate with 90's music, your favourite Geeta Dutt songs. You remember that song, 'Jane woh kaise, log they jinke pyar ko pyar mila' ('How, were those people, who gave love and received love in return')?"

With those closing words, I walked out of the house. Mom waved a hand, and I waved back to her. I was booking a cab when Shahid met me. He said, "That J was Jeeva, your manager. Right, Pooja? Maybe you didn't teach him how a manager should behave. But I will certainly show him how to treat a girl if you claim to love her."

I replied, "Shahid, it's not the way you are thinking."

Shahid smiled and asked, "May I drop you to the office?"

I said, "Sure."

I joined him on the pillion seat. Shahid turned on the music, and the song which he played was, 'Jane woh kaise log the jinke pyar ko pyar mila', the same song which I was planning to play for mom today. I told myself, "What a coincidence!"

Shahid dropped me to the office within 20 minutes.

"Pretty fast," I commented the moment we reached.

Shahid didn't say anything and drove the car away. I walked into the office. Everyone was talking about the riots in the office. But I didn't find J anywhere. I inquired about him. Unfortunately, he didn't tell it to anyone. J's manager, Mr. Deepak Majhi, called me in his cabin. I asked for his permission to join him in his cabin. He said, "Come in, Pooja. Take a seat."

I sat down saying, "Thank you so much, sir."

Deepak sir was in the middle of a call, I kept on staring at my phone screen. Deepak sir disconnected the call and said, "Yes, Miss Pooja. I have heard a lot about your work. You are making us proud. Are you happy with your 25% hike?"

I replied, "Yes, sir, I am satisfied with it."

"That's terrific. I just wanted to congratulate you personally. I wish you all the very best for your future," he ushered.

I said, "Thank you, sir, for trusting me so much. I will try my best to work in the best interest of TCL. Sir, one more thing, have you seen Mr. Jeeva in the office? I had to discuss something important with him."

"Oh, Jeeva is on leave for 1 week. Someone has died in his family. He has left for Meerut, as per my knowledge."

"Oh, so sorry for his loss. Never mind, I will talk to Sudarshan sir for the same." I left Mr. Deepak's cabin, thinking if J is out of the station then, why did he call me to the hotel?

Most probably, he must have lied to everyone. I was getting positive vibes about everything happening around me. A second wind was flowing inside me. I worked at the office till 3:30 PM. While I was packing up, Sakshi interrupted, "I see a different glow on your face. Are you going to get married soon?"

I chuckled, "Idiot! That was a good joke. I have no intentions of getting married anytime soon. But, yeah, I feel good today. Maybe that's why you felt so. Alright, I am leaving office. If anyone asks anything just tells that I wasn't feeling well."

"That I will say, but looks like you are going on a date," she joked.

I replied, "I would go on my first date only with you, my darling. Like you said earlier, if I don't get any guy, I will get married to you."

Both of us burst into laughter, and I left the office. I booked a cab after reaching downstairs to Holiday Inn and Suites. The cab was delayed by 5 minutes. I sat close to the exit gate. The phone rang. It was an SMS from an unknown number. I opened the text which read:

"Thank you for using our services. Please, spare 5 minutes to fill the feedback form."

I made faces and locked the cellphone. The cab had arrived. I boarded the cab. I also thought of calling J but dropped the idea. I wanted to seize the bull by the horns. The wait wasn't getting over. There were butterflies in my tummy. setting the Thames on fire. "No more shell games now. I will talk straight to the point," I explained to myself. Finally, I reached my destination. I ended the trip and walked inside the hotel. I asked for room no. 243, as mentioned in the note. The receptionist asked, "Whom do you wish to meet?"

I spoke hesitantly, "Mr. Jeeva."

The receptionist stared at me but then smiled saying, "Ma'am, please, have a seat while I confirm it with Mr. Jeeva. Please, wait for 5 minutes."

I said, "Yeah, sure."

I started waiting. By my watch, 3 minutes were over. I wanted her to call my name. And she called me exactly after 5 minutes, "Miss. Pooja, you can go. Mr. Jeeva has called you on the 5th level, which is the swimming pool level. Please, take a right and the first elevator to reach 5th level."

I nodded with a smile and entered the 5th level. J was standing in his favourite red shirt, facing the parking lot. I called him and he turned around to look at me.

He said, "Are you ok?"I replied, "Are you ok? I have to talk to you."

J replied, "Let's not talk here. I have a secret place. People can follow us. Even Satakshi has visited the same hotel for her cousin's wedding. I am scared that she might find us, walking in or out. In fact, she is also staying in the same hotel."

"Oh, but what did you tell Satakshi and why are you staying here?" I triggered a queue of questions.

"Too many questions to answer. Let's get out of this place in 5 minutes before Satakshi finds us."

I expressed concern, "Let's make haste."

J packed up from his room while I waited downstairs for him. We successfully landed in his car, and he drove it really soon to escape Satakshi. We are finally out of her reach.

"But where are we going?" I asked.

He replied, "To a secret place where just you and I can talk."

"I just need to talk to you for 5 minutes. An isolated place is not required for that," I yelled. Jeeva tried to calm me down, saying, "It's not safe for me to travel in public places. Police or any of their informers can identify me. I was caught on the camera in my car during the riots." "Even I saw your call on Television. You are in trouble J," I spoke sadly.

Jeeva assured that we will sort things out and all I need to do is to be patient for some time. Both of us were shooting from the hips. Never ever we had such an evolved and mature conversation.

"We have almost reached the place," J told me. "This is a terrible jungle. When did you find this place? No man or animal. Where are we?" I questioned in surprise.

"We are in the outskirts of greater Noida," J informed.

"Hmm... Ok. Let's talk first," I proposed.

J replied, "Before that, I want to kiss every part of your body. It's been so long since my organs met yours. This is a place where no one comes."

I said, "No, no, I don't want this."

J questioned, "What? You don't love me anymore? Just a day has changed everything between us?. All the love that we had."

"I want to talk to you first. Please, don't get me wrong, but I don't want all this."

J didn't listen to me and started pulling off my clothes, almost tearing them. I screamed, followed by which we heard a police hooter. J said, "Shit, Pooja, wear your clothes back. Let's get out of here first."J drove the car back to the mainroad, peeping for the police in the rear mirror.

"Where should we go? I have to see you properly for 5 minutes," he said.

I answered, "Let's go to your home. Since it's 14th August, today, the police are on high alert. Your wife and children are not at home. Let's go and talk there. Listen J, I don't want to get physical with you, but I need to know what did you tell my mom so that I can win her trust back."

J agreed and drove back to his home. Later, we didn't find any police jeep following us. We took a breath of relief. I was sick as a parrot with the behaviour of J. I decided to stay away from him, telling him that this is in the common interest of both the families. We didn't speak until the moment we reached home. The distance was of 45 minutes but felt like 5 minutes. The clock had struck 12:00 and we entered into a new day. Running from 3:30 PM to 12 AM was a tedious job.

Both of us were six feet under our thoughts about what has been happening with us. This was the last slam drum of our lives. After this, I wanted to sleep like a baby in my mother's lap with new independence. J parked the car in his apartment, and I moved to the 5th floor of his apartment building. Co-incidentally, his apartment was 555. The moment he was unlocking the door, I commented, "Since the time I met you, this figure '5' has stuck to me like an evil's eye. There were a lot of slippery slopes, telling me that those 5 minutes will leave you with the last 5 minutes of your life, but I treated all the warning like squaring the circle."

It felt like somebody was on the floor, there was a commotion. J pushed me inside the house and didn't close the door to make things look normal. Crossing the drawing-room, we entered the bedroom. The bedroom was decorated with J's both individual and family pictures. There were a lot of butterflies flying on the wall canvas, and a mini-fridge was installed inside the room, to give the room a bar-like feel. I said, "Good one, J, well decorated."

J was getting aroused. He hugged me and said, "Pooja, I need you."

I pushed him with my arms and said, "J, listen to this."

He removed his shirt and sucked my lips with his before I could say anything. He tore my t-shirt, pulling it off with all his strength. I repeated, "J, listen to me. I don't want this. Please. I don't want to scream."

He didn't listen to me and pulled down my skirt, tearing that off too.

"J… J… J… please, first talk to me. Stop dancing on your erections."

J didn't listen to me. I tried pushing him back, but he pulled me towards him, kissing my neck and not letting me go. I wasn't enjoying it and suddenly, I felt some liquid oozing out of J's stomach.

I said, "Please, control your excitement. It's not the time to grow harder or tighter."

J fell on his back and my hands were colored red. J was bathing in blood. I shouted. I was about to check for J's heartbeats, but suddenly something hit my head in deep silence. I fell on the left side of my body, shivering and unable to understand what has happened. Just 5 minutes back, we were sorting things out. What happened suddenly? I touched my head and saw a lot of blood around. I tried to look for the person who shot the bullet with my flapping eyes. I saw mom and Shahid standing together. Mom was struggling to reach me and Shahid was holding her back, asking her to get out from the place. It felt like I was left with the last 5 minutes to watch both of them. Just 5 minutes to tell them how much I loved them. 5 minutes to make them understand that I wasn't wrong. I needed just 5 minutes more to finish everything and get back to my old world. For 5 minutes, I wanted to hug my mother tight and tell her that I loved her more than anything in my life. Shahid managed to escape with mother. I wanted them to run away. I dragged myself closer to J, asking for his forgiveness as he was going to die because of me. "J, You wanted me to stay with you. Right? I knew I won't be able to be with you because we are so different, but my love for you was true. I never wanted to get physically attached, rather emotionally. My commitment to you was genuine and see, I am dying with you in your house. In the same house where you live. Where you imagined to welcome me at some point of time. Today, I am speaking to God, asking him to rewind my life a little to know what my mother and Shahid think about me. I have closed my eyes, trying to join the dots and almighty is helping me with this.

That note, which I recieved from the washer man was not from J, but from mom. Mom had sent a similar note to J, so that we meet and she can understand who is tormenting her daughter. With the difference in statement of both J and Shahid, mom undertsood that none of them were speaking the truth. Mom took offs on both the days to check the CCTV footage of the parking lot and also contacted the person who made the video at the time of the riots. She could understand the entire scene just by watching the complete video, which had J, Shahid and I, the three of us. Mom followed me right from the office to every place I visited. Shahid bribed the Vodafone operators in order to track Jeeva's location. Shahid took Jeeva's number the next morning, after the riots, when he came to see me.. Mom even asked Shahid why he wanted the number, which Shahid ignored by saying, "I have to give it to some friend for some interview purpose."

The benefit of the doubt turned postive in mom for Jeeva. Shahid dropped the service feedback message to get my location. Shahid followed us, too, at every location. The hooter was not the Police's jeep, but a false alarm rung by Shahid to save me. When J was opening the door, the bustling noise was not of the cat's but of mom and Shahid hiding from each other. Both realised about each other's presence. When J was getting horny in the bedroom, mom hid in his kitchen, followed by Shahid, who was hiding in the common washroom between the drawing room and bedroom. While J was tearing off my clothes, Shahid managed to enter the bedroom and stabbed J in the back. 10 seconds later, mom tried to shoot Jeeva with a local pistol. But since he fell before the bullet reached him, it struck my head. I was accidently killed. Mother tried to reach me, but Shahid stopped her from doing that as she could have been given the death penalty for killing her own daughter. He kept her away, so that no evidences can be found against her. He picked the gun and forced mom to go outside the building, driving her back home while she kept on shouting and struggling to apologise to me and hug me for the last time. She wanted to save me, but guess that's not what destiny wanted. I took my last breath in gratification. Both Shahid and mom loved me more than their lives and hence they risked everything to pluck the thorns of my life; the thorns which I sowed on my own. I wasn't a weak woman, but the love inside me for J made me weak. And, the weak has to die. That's what Darwin's theory of the 'Survival of the fittest says'. Loving someone, at times turns out to be your greatest strength and sometimes, your biggest failure. I finally closed my eyes, thanking God for stemming the tide of regret and helping me to understand the sticky wicket. I can now, finally, rest in peace. Thank you mom for giving me wings. It was only you who taught me to fly. You are my attitude, please, let it always stay high. I took my last breath in the name of Ma.

No evidences were found against Mom and Shahid. Shahid had already deactivated the CCTV cameras of the society using a still virus. The case was closed concluding, "Some intruders had entered the house by force and tried to molest the girl and the man revolted. As a result of which, the man was stabbed. Since the girl started shouting after seeing the man dead, the thieves shot her dead too. The police are in search of those thieves, the knife and the pistol. Both the knife and the pistol have vanished from the crime scene. Shahid threw them in the holy river, Ganga, on their way back to Varanasi.

Today, both Shahid and mom run a defence academy for girls where they empower girls with latest fighting skills. Government has also started supporting them in strengthening the female population of India. The name of the defence academy is 'Pooja Defence Academy'. My photo stands tall in a frame in the main office of the academy, honoured by a garland. I feel proud of my friend Shahid and my mother for doing such a generous work. I hope to one day come back again as Shahid's friend and my mom's daughter and learn to fight even in love.